PE

ABSURD DRAMA

ABSURD DRAMA

AMÉDÉE OR HOW TO GET RID OF IT
Eugène Ionesco

PROFESSOR TARANNE
Arthur Adamov

THE TWO EXECUTIONERS
Fernando Arrabal

THE ZOO STORY
Edward Albee
(*This play published in association with Jonathan Cape*)

WITH AN INTRODUCTION BY
MARTIN ESSLIN

PENGUIN BOOKS

Penguin Books Ltd, Harmondsworth, Middlesex, England
Penguin Books Pty Ltd, Ringwood, Victoria, Australia

—

Amédée or How to Get Rid of it
Copyright © Ionesco/Gallimard 1956
This translation first published by John Calder 1958
Copyright © John Calder (Publishers) Ltd, 1958

—

Professor Taranne
Copyright © Arthur Adamov, 1962
This translation first published by John Calder 1962
Copyright © Peter Meyer and Derek Prouse, 1962

—

The Two Executioners
Copyright © René Juilliard, 1958
This translation first published by John Calder 1962
Copyright © John Calder (Publishers) Ltd, 1962

—

The Zoo Story
First published in Great Britain by Jonathan Cape 1962
Copyright © Edward Albee 1960 and 1961

—

Published in Penguin Books 1965
Made and printed in Great Britain by C. Nicholls & Company Ltd
Set in Monotype Baskerville

CONTENTS

INTRODUCTION

'The Theatre of the Absurd' has become a catch-phrase, much used and much abused. What does it stand for? And how can such a label be justified? Perhaps it will be best to attempt to answer the second question first. There is no organized movement, no school of artists, who claim the label for themselves. A good many playwrights who have been classed under this label, when asked if they *belong* to the Theatre of the Absurd, will indignantly reply that they belong to no such movement – and quite rightly so. For each of the playwrights concerned seeks to express no more and no less than his own personal vision of the world.

Yet critical concepts of this kind are useful when new modes of expression, new conventions of art arise. When the plays of Ionesco, Beckett, Genet, and Adamov first appeared on the stage they puzzled and outraged most critics as well as audiences. And no wonder. These plays flout all the standards by which drama has been judged for many centuries; they must therefore appear as a provocation to people who have come into the theatre expecting to find what they would recognize as a well-made play. A well-made play is expected to present characters that are well-observed and convincingly motivated: these plays often contain hardly any recognizable human beings and present completely unmotivated actions. A well-made play is expected to entertain by the ding-dong of witty and logically built-up dialogue: in some of these plays dialogue seems to have degenerated into meaningless babble. A well-made play is expected to have a beginning, a middle, and a neatly tied-up ending: these plays often start at an arbitrary point and seem to end just as arbitrarily. By all the traditional standards of critical appreciation of the drama, these plays are not only abominably bad, they do not even deserve the name of drama.

And yet, strangely enough, these plays have *worked*, they have had an effect, they have exercised a fascination of their own in the theatre. At first it was said that this fascination was merely a *succès de scandale*, that people flocked to see Beckett's *Waiting for Godot* or Ionesco's *Bald Primadonna* merely because it had become fashionable to be able to express outrage and astonishment about them at parties. But this explanation clearly could not apply to more than one or two plays of this kind. And the success of a whole row of similarly unconventional works became more and more manifest. If the critical touchstones of traditional drama did not apply to these plays, this must surely have been due to a difference in objective, the use of different artistic means, to the fact, in short, that these plays were both creating and applying a different *convention* of drama. It is just as senseless to condemn an abstract painting because it lacks perspective or a recognizable subject-matter as it is to reject *Waiting for Godot* because it has no plot to speak of. In painting a composition of squares and lines an artist like Mondrian does not *want* to depict any object in nature, he does not *want* to create perspective. Similarly, in writing *Waiting for Godot* Beckett did not intend to tell a story, he did not *want* the audience to go home satisfied that they knew the solution to the problem posed in the play. Hence there is no point in reproaching him with not doing what he never sought to do; the only reasonable course is to try and find out what it was that he did intend.

Yet, if tackled directly most of the playwrights in question would refuse to discuss any theories or objectives behind their work. They would, with perfect justification, point out that they are concerned with one thing only: to express their vision of the world as best they can, simply because, as artists, they feel an irrepressible urge to do so. This is where the critic can step in. By describing the works that do not fit into the established convention, by bringing out the similarities of approach in a number of more or less obviously related new works, by analysing the nature of their method and their artistic effect, he can try to define the framework of the new convention, and by doing so, can provide the standards by

8

which it will become possible to have works in that convention meaningfully compared and evaluated. The onus of proof that there is such a convention involved clearly lies on the critic, but if he can establish that there are basic similarities in approach, he can argue that these similarities must arise from common factors in the experience of the writers concerned. And these common factors must in turn spring from the spiritual climate of our age (which no sensitive artist can escape) and also perhaps from a common background of artistic influences, a similarity of roots, a shared tradition.

A term like the Theatre of the Absurd must therefore be understood as a kind of intellectual shorthand for a complex pattern of similarities in approach, method, and convention, of shared philosophical and artistic premises, whether conscious or subconscious, and of influences from a common store of tradition. A label of this kind therefore is an aid to understanding, valid only in so far as it helps to gain insight into a work of art. It is not a binding classification; it is certainly not all-embracing or exclusive. A play may contain *some* elements that can best be understood in the light of such a label, while other elements in the same play derive from and can best be understood in the light of a different convention. Arthur Adamov, for example, has written a number of plays that are prime examples of the Theatre of the Absurd. He now quite openly and consciously rejects this style and writes in a different, realistic convention. Nevertheless even his latest plays, which are both realistic and socially committed, contain some aspects which can still be elucidated in terms of the Theatre of the Absurd (such as the use of symbolic interludes, *guignols*, in his play *Spring '71*). Moreover, once a a term like Theatre of the Absurd is defined and understood, it acquires a certain value in throwing light on works of previous epochs. The Polish critic Jan Kott, for example, has written a brilliant study of *King Lear* in the light of Beckett's *Endgame*. And that this was no vain academic exercise but a genuine aid to understanding is shown by the fact that Peter

Brook's great production of *King Lear* took many of its ideas from Kott's essay.

What then *is* the convention of drama that has now acquired the label of the Theatre of the Absurd?

Let us take one of the plays in this volume as a starting point: Ionesco's *Amédée*. A middle-aged husband and wife are shown in a situation which is clearly not taken from real life. They have not left their flat for years. The wife earns her living by operating some sort of telephone switchboard; the husband is writing a play, but has never got beyond the first few lines. In the bedroom is a corpse. It has been there for many years. It may be the corpse of the wife's lover whom the husband killed when he found them together, but this is by no means certain; it may also have been a burglar, or a stray visitor. But the oddest thing about it is that it keeps growing larger and larger; it is suffering from 'geometric progression, the incurable disease of the dead'. And in the course of the play it grows so large that eventually an enormous foot bursts from the bedroom into the living-room, threatening to drive Amédée and his wife out of their home. All this is wildly fantastic, yet it is not altogether unfamiliar, for it is not unlike situations most of us have experienced at one time or another in dreams and nightmares.

Ionesco has in fact put a dream situation onto the stage, and in a dream quite clearly the rules of realistic theatre no longer apply. Dreams do not develop logically; they develop by association. Dreams do not communicate ideas; they communicate images. And indeed the growing corpse in *Amédée* can best be understood as a poetic image. It is in the nature both of dreams and of poetic imagery that they are ambiguous and carry a multitude of meanings at one and the same time, so that it is futile to ask what the image of the growing corpse stands for. On the other hand one can say that the corpse *might* evoke the growing power of past mistakes or past guilt, perhaps the waning of love or the death of affection – some evil in any case that festers and grows worse with time. The image can stand for any and all of these ideas, and its ability to embrace them all gives it the poetic power it undoubtedly possesses.

Not all the plays of the Theatre of the Absurd can be defined simply as dreams (although Adamov's *Professor Taranne* in this volume actually came to Adamov as a dream, Albee's *Zoo Story* is clearly far more firmly anchored in reality) but in all of them the poetic image is the focus of interest. In other words: while most plays in the traditional convention are primarily concerned to tell a story or elucidate an intellectual problem, and can thus be seen as a narrative or discursive form of communication, the plays of the Theatre of the Absurd are primarily intended to convey a poetic image or a complex pattern of poetic images; they are above all a poetical form. Narrative or discursive thought proceeds in a dialectical manner and must lead to a result or final message; it is therefore dynamic and moves along a definite line of development. Poetry is above all concerned to convey its central idea, or atmosphere, or mode of being; it is essentially static.

This does not mean, however, that these plays lack movement: the movement in *Amédée*, for instance, is relentless, lying as it does in the pressure of the ever-growing corpse. But the situation of the play remains static; the movement we see is that of the unfolding of the poetic image. The more ambiguous and complex that image, the more intricate and intriguing will be the process of revealing it. That is why a play like *Waiting for Godot* can generate considerable suspense and dramatic tension in spite of being a play in which literally *nothing* happens, a play designed to show that nothing *can* ever happen in human life. It is only when the last lines have been spoken and the curtain has fallen that we are in a position to grasp the total pattern of the complex poetic image we have been confronted with. If, in the traditional play, the action goes from point A to point B, and we constantly ask, 'what's going to happen next?', here we have an action that consists in the gradual unfolding of a complex pattern, and instead we ask, 'what is it that we are seeing?

What will the completed image be when we have grasped the nature of the pattern?' Thus in Arrabal's *The Two Executioners* in this volume we realize at the end of the play that the theme is the exploration of a complex image of the mother–son relationship; in Albee's *Zoo Story* it is only in the last lines of the play that the idea of the entire dialogue between Jerry and Peter falls into place, as an image of the difficulty of communication between human beings in our world.

Why should the emphasis in drama have shifted away from traditional forms towards images which, complex and suggestive as they may be, must necessarily lack the final clarity of definition, the neat resolutions we have been used to expect? Clearly because the playwrights concerned no longer believe in the possibility of such neatness of resolution. They are indeed chiefly concerned with expressing a sense of wonder, of incomprehension, and at times of despair, at the lack of cohesion and meaning that they find in the world. If they could believe in clearly defined motivations, acceptable solutions, settlement of conflict in tidily tied up endings, these dramatists would certainly not eschew them. But, quite obviously, they have no faith in the existence of so rational and well ordered a universe. The 'well-made play' can thus be seen as conditioned by clear and comforting beliefs, a stable scale of values, an ethical system in full working condition. The system of values, the world-view behind the well-made play may be a religious one or a political one; it may be an implicit belief in the goodness and perfectibility of man (as in Shaw or Ibsen) or it may be a mere unthinking acceptance of the moral and political status quo (as in most drawing-room comedy). But whatever it is, the basis of the well-made play is the implicit assumption that the world does make sense, that reality is solid and secure, all outlines clear, all ends apparent. The plays that we have classed under the label of the Theatre of the Absurd, on the other hand, express a sense of shock at the absence, the loss of any such clear and well-defined systems of beliefs or values.

There can be little doubt that such a sense of disillusionment, such a collapse of all previously held firm beliefs is a characteristic feature of our own times. The social and spiritual reasons for such a sense of loss of meaning are manifold and complex: the waning of religious faith that had started with the Enlightenment and led Nietzsche to speak of the 'death of God' by the eighteen-eighties; the breakdown of the liberal faith in inevitable social progress in the wake of the First World War; the disillusionment with the hopes of radical social revolution as predicted by Marx after Stalin had turned the Soviet Union into a totalitarian tyranny; the relapse into barbarism, mass murder, and genocide in the course of Hitler's brief rule over Europe during the Second World War; and, in the aftermath of that war, the spread of spiritual emptiness in the outwardly prosperous and affluent societies of Western Europe and the United States. There can be no doubt: for many intelligent and sensitive human beings the world of the mid twentieth century *has* lost its meaning and has simply ceased to make sense. Previously held certainties have dissolved, the firmest foundations for hope and optimism have collapsed. Suddenly man sees himself faced with a universe that is both frightening and illogical – in a word, absurd. All assurances of hope, all explanations of ultimate meaning have suddenly been unmasked as nonsensical illusions, empty chatter, whistling in the dark. If we try to imagine such a situation in ordinary life, this might amount to our suddenly ceasing to understand the conversation in a room full of people; what made sense at one moment has, at the next, become an obscure babble of voices in a foreign language. At once the comforting, familiar scene would turn into one of nightmare and horror. With the loss of the means of communication we should be compelled to view that world with the eyes of total outsiders as a succession of frightening images.

Such a sense of loss of meaning must inevitably lead to a questioning of the recognized instrument for the *communication* of meaning: language. Consequently the Theatre of the Absurd is to a very considerable extent concerned with a critique of language, an attack above all on fossilized forms of language which have become devoid of meaning. The conversation at the party which at one moment *seemed* to be an exchange of information about the weather, or new books, or the respective health of the participants, is suddenly revealed as an exchange of mere meaningless banalities. The people talking about the weather had no intention whatever of really exchanging meaningful information on the subject; they were merely using language to fill the emptiness between them, to conceal the fact that they had no desire to tell each other anything at all. In other words, from being a noble instrument of genuine communication language has become a kind of ballast filling empty spaces. And equally, in a universe that seems to be drained of meaning, the pompous and laborious attempts at explanation that we call philosophy or politics must appear as empty chatter. In *Waiting for Godot* for example Beckett parodies and mocks the language of philosophy and science in Lucky's famous speech. Harold Pinter, whose uncanny accuracy in the reproduction of real conversation among English people has earned him the reputation of having a tape-recorder built into his memory, reveals that the bulk of everyday conversation is largely devoid of logic and sense, is in fact nonsensical. It is at this point that the Theatre of the Absurd can actually coincide with the highest degree of realism. For if the real conversation of human beings is in fact absurd and nonsensical, then it is the well-made play with its polished logical dialogue that is unrealistic, while the absurdist play may well be a tape-recorded reproduction of reality. Or, in a world that has become absurd, the Theatre of the Absurd is the most realistic comment on, the most accurate reproduction of, reality.

In its critique of language the Theatre of the Absurd closely reflects the preoccupation of contemporary philosophy with language, its effort to disentangle language, as a genuine instrument for logic and the discovery of reality, from the welter of emotive, illogical usages, the grammatical

conventions that have, in the past, often been confused with
genuine logical relationships. And equally, in its emphasis
on the basic absurdity of the human condition, on the bank-
ruptcy of all closed systems of thought with claims to provide
a total explanation of reality, the Theatre of the Absurd has
much in common with the existential philosophy of Heideg-
ger, Sartre, and Camus. (It was in fact Camus who coined
the concept of the Absurd in the sense in which it is used here.)
This is not to say that the dramatists of the Absurd are trying
to translate contemporary philosophy into drama. It is
merely that philosophers and dramatists respond to the same
cultural and spiritual situation and reflect the same pre-
occupations.

Yet, however contemporary the Theatre of the Absurd
may appear it is by no means the revolutionary novelty as
which some of its champions, as well as some of its bitterest
critics, tend to represent it. In fact the Theatre of the Absurd
can best be understood as a new combination of a number of
ancient, even archaic, traditions of literature and drama. It
is surprising and shocking merely because of the unusual
nature of the combination and the increased emphasis on
aspects of drama that, while present in all plays, rarely
emerge into the foreground.

The ancient traditions combined in a new form in the
Theatre of the Absurd are: the tradition of miming and
clowning that goes back to the *mimus* of Greece and Rome, the
commedia dell' arte of Renaissance Italy, and such popular
forms of theatre as the pantomime or the music-hall in
Britain; the equally ancient tradition of nonsense poetry; the
tradition of dream and nightmare literature that also goes
back to Greek and Roman times; allegorical and symbolic
drama, such as we find it in medieval morality plays, or in
the Spanish *auto sacramental*; the ancient tradition of fools and
mad scenes in drama, of which Shakespeare provides a
multitude of examples; and the even more ancient tradition
of ritual drama that goes back to the very origins of the
theatre where religion and drama were still one. It is no

coincidence that one of the masters of the Theatre of the Absurd, Jean Genet, regards his plays as attempts at re-capturing the ritual element in the Mass itself, which, after all, can be seen as a poetic image of an archetypal event brought to life through a sequence of symbolical actions.

It is against this background that we must see the history of the movement which culminates in Beckett, Ionesco, or Genet. Its immediate forebears are dramatists like Strind-berg, who progressed from photographic naturalism to more and more openly expressionist representations of dreams, nightmares, or obsessions in plays like the *Ghost Sonata*, *Dream Play*, or *To Damascus*, and novelists like James Joyce and Kafka. A form of drama concerned with dream-like imagery and the failure of language was bound to find inspira-tion also in the silent cinema, with its dream-like quality and cruel, sometimes nightmare humour. Charlie Chaplin's little man and Buster Keaton's stonefaced stoic are among the openly acknowledged influences of writers like Beckett and Ionesco. These comedians, after all, derive from the most ancient tradition of clowning, as do, in the talking cinema, the Marx Brothers, W. C. Fields, or Laurel and Hardy, all clearly part of the tradition which leads to the Theatre of the Absurd.

Another direct and acknowledged influence is that of the Dadaists, the surrealists, and the Parisian avant-garde that derives from writers like Alfred Jarry (1873–1907) and Guillaume Apollinaire (1880–1918). Jarry's *Ubu Roi*, first performed in 1896, might in fact be called the first modern example of the Theatre of the Absurd. It is a savage farce in which monstrous puppets castigate the greed and emptiness of bourgeois society through a series of grotesque stage images. Apollinaire's play *Les Mamelles de Tiresias* ('The Breasts of Tiresias') was the first play to be labelled by its author as 'a surrealist drama'. Here too the action proceeds through a series of savagely grotesque images; the hero, or rather the heroine, Thérèse-Tiresias changes sex by letting her breasts float towards the heavens in the shape of two toy balloons. Jarry and Apollinaire were the direct precursors of the Dadaists in Switzerland, France, and Germany. Brecht's earliest plays bear the marks of Dadaist influence and can be regarded as early examples of the Theatre of the Absurd: *In the Jungle of the Cities* for instance presents the audience with a totally unmotivated struggle, a series of poetic images of man fighting a senseless battle with himself. In France the two leading exponents of surrealism in drama were Antonin Artaud (1896–1948) and Roger Vitrac (1899–1952). Vitrac's play *Victor ou Les Enfants au Pouvoir* (1924) anticipates Ionesco and Arrabal by showing the world from the point of view of a nine-year-old child of giant size and monstrous intelligence. Artaud, who wrote very little in dramatic form himself, is of immense importance as a theoretician of the new anti-literary theatre: he coined the slogan of the 'Theatre of Cruelty' for his conception of a theatre designed to shock its audience into a full awareness of the horror of the human condition. Jean-Louis Barrault and Roger Blin, two of the leading directors of the contemporary avant-garde theatre, were pupils of Artaud; Arthur Adamov was among his closest friends.

In its present form the Theatre of the Absurd is a post-war phenomenon. Genet's *The Maids* had its first performance at the Athénée in Paris in 1947; Ionesco's *Bald Primadonna* and Adamov's earliest plays were first produced in 1950; Beckett's *Waiting for Godot* in 1952. It will be noticed that all these first performances took place in Paris. And Paris certainly is the fountainhead of the Theatre of the Absurd. Yet it is equally strange and significant that the playwrights themselves are largely exiles from other countries domiciled in Paris: Beckett (born 1906) an Anglo-Irishman who writes in French; Ionesco (born 1912) half-French and half-Rumanian; Adamov (born 1908) a Russo-Armenian. Only Genet is a Frenchman born and bred, but then he is an exile in a different sense: an exile from society itself, a child abandoned by his mother, brought up by foster-parents and drifting from detention centres for juvenile delinquents into an underworld of thieves and male prostitutes, prison and penitentiary. It is in the experience of the outcast or exile that our image of the world seen from the outside assumes a new and added significance: for the exile, from his country or from society, moves in a world drained of meaning, sees people in pursuit of objectives he cannot comprehend, hears them speak a language that he cannot follow. The exile's basic experience is the archetype and the anticipation of twentieth-century man's shock at his realization that the world is ceasing to make sense.

Of the dramatists of the Absurd Samuel Beckett is undoubtedly the profoundest, the greatest poet. *Waiting for Godot* and *Endgame* are certainly masterpieces; *Happy Days* and *Play, Krapp's Last Tape*, and the two *Acts without Words* (where language has drained away altogether) are brilliant and profound poetic images; and the radio plays *All that Fall, Embers, Words and Music*, and *Cascando* have an equal enigmatic power.

Jean Genet (born 1910) lacks Beckett's discipline, intellect, and erudition, but he too is a poet, endowed with the well-nigh magic power of creating beauty from evil, corruption, and excrement. If the evanescence of man in time and the mystery of human personality and identity are Beckett's main themes, Genet's chief concern is with the falseness of human pretensions in society, the contrast between appearance and reality, which itself must remain for ever elusive. In *The Maids* we see the servants bound in a mixture of hatred and erotic dependence to their mistress, re-enacting this love-hate in an endless series of ritual games; in *The Balcony* society itself is symbolized in the image of a brothel providing its customers with the illusions of power; and in *The Blacks* we are back with the underdog acting out his hatred for his oppressor (which is also a form of love) in an endless ritual of mock-murder.

Jean Tardieu (born 1903) and Boris Vian (1920–59) are among the best of the French dramatists of the Absurd. Tardieu is an experimenter who has systematically explored

the possibilities of a theatre that can divorce itself from discursive speech to the point where language becomes mere
musical sound. Vian, a devoted follower of Jarry, wrote a
play, *The Empire Builders*, which shows man fleeing from
death and loneliness in the image of a family moving into
ever smaller flats on higher and higher floors of a mysterious
building.

In Italy Dino Buzzati and Ezio d'Errico, in Germany
Günter Grass (known as a novelist for his monumental *Tin
Drum*) and Wolfgang Hildesheimer are the main exponents
of the Theatre of the Absurd. In Britain N. F. Simpson,
James Saunders, David Campton, and Harold Pinter might
be classed under this heading. N. F. Simpson has clear links
with English nonsense literature, Lewis Carroll and Edward
Lear. James Saunders, particularly in *Next Time I'll Sing to
You*, expresses in dramatic form the thought of the existen-
tialist philosophers. Pinter, who acknowledges Kafka and
Beckett among his literary heroes, combines realism with an
intuition of the absurdity of human existence. In his later
work he has shed some of the allegorical symbolism of his
beginnings, but even in seemingly realistic plays like *The
Collection* there is an absence of motivation and solution, a
multiple ambiguity and a sense of non-communication which
transforms the seemingly realistic account of humdrum
adultery into a poetic image of the human condition.

Behind the Iron Curtain, where socialist realism is the
official creed in the theatre, there would appear to be no
room for an avant-garde trend of this type. Yet there is one
country where the influence of the Theatre of the Absurd has
produced some astonishngly successful plays: Poland, an
area of relative artistic freedom since the defeat of the Stalin-
ists by Gomulka in the autumn of 1956. A strong surrealist
influence was present in Poland even before the war (Gom-
browicz and Witkiewicz are two dramatists who might be
regarded as among the most important immediate precursors of the Theatre of the Absurd) so that the soil was fertile
for a development which was further fostered by the ability

of drama of this kind to express political comment in a suitably oblique form. A number of young dramatists, notably Slawomir Mrozek and Tadeusz Rozewicz, have produced outstandingly original work in the convention of the Absurd.

Three of the playwrights represented in this volume are Parisian exiles. Eugène Ionesco is undoubtedly the most fertile and original of the dramatists of the Absurd, and also, in spite of a streak of clowning and fun for its own sake in his work, one of the most profound. He is moreover the most vocal of the dramatists of the Absurd, the only one who is prepared to discuss the theoretical foundations of his work and to reply to the attacks on it from committed left-wing realists. The critique of language and the haunting presence of death are Ionesco's chief themes in plays like *The Bald Primadonna, The Lesson, The Chairs, The Killer, Rhinoceros,* and *Exit the King. Amédée or How to Get Rid of It* (1953) is Ionesco's first full-length play and contains one of his most telling images. It is also characteristic in its alternation between states of depression and euphoria, leaden oppression and floating on air, an image which reappears through his work and which culminates, in this particular play, in Amédée's floating away at the end.

Arthur Adamov today belongs to the camp against which Ionesco directs his harshest polemics, the socialist realists whose organ is the periodical *Théâtre populaire,* but he started out as a follower of Artaud, a self-confessed neurotic, an alien in a senseless world. Adamov's development from one extreme to the other is a fascinating artistic and psychological case history, in which *Professor Taranne* occupies a key position. Adamov's progress can be seen as a process of psychological therapy through writing. Unable to face the reality of the outside world, he started out by projecting his oppressions and anxieties on to the stage. Nothing would have induced him, he has since confessed, to mention any element of the real world, such as a place-name in one of his plays; he would have regarded that as a piece of unspeakable vulgarity. And yet, when he committed to paper the dream which is now the play *Professor Taranne*, he realized that a real place name, that of Belgium, had occurred in the dream. Truthfulness in transcribing the dream thus forced him to compromise on one of his fundamental artistic principles. And from then onwards reality kept breaking through into his writing in ever more insistent form, until today he is a thorough-going realist of the Brechtian school. That is to say, by writing his obsessions out of his system Adamov acquired the ability to face and to control the objective world from which he had withdrawn into neurosis. It might be argued that the projection of neurotic obsessions is both more interesting and more illuminating in providing insights into the dark side of the human mind than the accurate transcription of historical events, and that therefore Adamov's absurdist plays are more fascinating, more successful than his later efforts. But this is a matter of taste as well as of ideological bias. The fact remains that *Professor Taranne* and the somewhat more realistic *Ping Pong* are undoubtedly among Adamov's best plays.

Fernando Arrabal (born 1932) is a Spaniard who has been living in France since 1954 and now writes in French. He is an admirer of Beckett, but sees his roots in the surrealist tradition of Spain, a country that has always been rich in fantasy and the grotesque (El Greco, Goya) and that in more recent times has produced such outstanding representatives of the modern movement as the painter Picasso (who has himself written two plays in an absurdist vein) and the writers Lorca and Valle Inclàn. Arrabal's own contribution to the absurdist spectrum is a highly original one: his main preoccupation is with the absurdity of ethical and moral rules. He looks at the world with the incomprehension of a child that simply cannot understand the logic of conventional morality. Thus, in *The Automobile Graveyard* there is a prostitute who follows her profession simply because religion demands that one be kind to one's neighbours; how then could she refuse them the ultimate kindness of giving herself to them? And similarly in *The Two Executioners* the rebel son who objects to the tortures that his mother inflicts on his father is faced with the dilemma of several contradictory moral laws: obedience to one's father, the human goodness that prompts one to save the suffering victim from his torturers, and the need to honour and obey one's mother. These moral laws are here in obvious conflict, as it is the mother who has the father tortured. Clearly the situation in which several moral laws are in contradiction exposes the absurdity of the system of values that accommodates them all. Arrabal refuses to judge; he merely notes the position and shows that he finds it beyond his comprehension.

Edward Albee (born 1928) is one of the few American exponents of the Theatre of the Absurd. An adopted child, he shares with Genet the orphan's sense of loneliness in an alien world; and the image of the dream child which exists only in the adoptive parents' imagination recurs in a number of his plays, notably *The American Dream* and *Who's Afraid of Virginia Woolf*. The latter, which has earned him an enormous success on Broadway, is undoubtedly one of the finest American plays since the heyday of Eugene O'Neill. It is a savage dance of death reminiscent of Strindberg, outwardly realistic in form, but in fact, as in the case of Pinter's best work, existing on at least two levels apart from the realistic one: as an allegory of American society, a poetic image of its emptiness and sterility, and as a complex ritual on the pattern of Genet. *The Zoo Story* (1958), one of Albee's earliest dramatic ventures, has a similar complexity: it is a clinically accurate study of schizophrenia, an image of man's loneliness and inability to make contact, and also, on the ritual and symbolic level, an act of ritual self-immolation that has curious parallels with Christ's atonement. (Note the names Jerry – Jesus? – and Peter).

The plays in this volume, like the plays of the Theatre of the Absurd in general, present a disillusioned, harsh, and stark picture of the world. Though often couched in the form of extravagant fantasies, they are nevertheless essentially realistic, in the sense that they never shirk the realities of the human mind with its despair, fear and loneliness in an alien and hostile universe. There is more human reality in the grotesquely extravagant images of *Amédée* than in many far longer plays in a convention that is a mere photographic copy of the surface of life. The realism of these plays is a psychological, and inner realism; they explore the human subconscious in depth rather than trying to describe the outward appearance of human existence. Nor is it quite correct that these plays, deeply pessimistic as they are, are nothing but an expression of utter despair. It is true that basically the Theatre of the Absurd attacks the comfortable certainties of religious or political orthodoxy. It aims to shock its audience out of complacency, to bring it face to face with the harsh facts of the human situation as these writers see it. But the challenge behind this message is anything but one of despair. It is a challenge to accept the human condition as it is, in all its mystery and absurdity, and to bear it with dignity, nobly, responsibly; precisely *because* there are no easy solutions to the mysteries of existence, because ultimately man is alone in a meaningless world. The shedding of easy solutions, of comforting illusions, may be painful, but it leaves behind it a sense of freedom and relief. And that is why, in the last resort, the Theatre of the Absurd does not provoke tears of despair but the laughter of liberation.

EUGÈNE IONESCO

AMÉDÉE

OR

How to Get Rid of it

A COMEDY
Translated by Donald Watson

AMÉDÉE
or How to Get Rid of it

A COMEDY

First produced in Paris by Jean-Marie Serreau at the Théâtre de Babylone, 14 April 1954

First performed in England at the Arts Theatre, Cambridge, on 3 June 1957
Producer, Peter Zadek

CHARACTERS

AMÉDÉE BUCCINIONI, aged forty-five
MADELEINE, his wife, aged forty-five
(AMÉDÉE II)
(MADELEINE II)
A POSTMAN
FIRST AMERICAN SOLDIER
(SECOND AMERICAN SOLDIER)
MADO, a girl
(THE OWNER of the bar)
FIRST POLICEMAN
SECOND POLICEMAN
A MAN at the window
A WOMAN at the window

ACT ONE

———◆———

Scene: An unpretentious dining-room, drawing-room, and office combined.
On the right, a door.
On the left, another door.
Backstage centre, a large window with closed shutters; the space between the slats is, however, wide enough to let in sufficient light.
Left centre, a small table strewn with notebooks and pencils. On the right, against the wall, between the window and the right-hand door, a small table, with a telephone switchboard on it, and a chair. Another chair also close to the centre table. An old armchair well down stage. There should be no other furniture in the first act, except a clearly visible clock, with hands that move.

[*As the curtain rises* AMÉDÉE BUCCINIONI *is walking nervously round and about the furniture, with his head bent and his hands clasped behind his back, thinking hard. He is of middle age, a* petit bourgeois, *preferably bald, with a small greying moustache, wearing spectacles, dressed in a dark jacket and black striped trousers, a butterfly collar and black tie. Every now and again he goes to the centre table, opens a notebook, picks up a pencil, and tries to write (he is a playwright); but he has no success, or writes, perhaps, one word which he at once crosses out. It is obvious that he is not at ease: he is also casting occasional glances at the door on the left, which is half open. His anxiety and nervousness are steadily growing. While he is walking round the room, his eyes fixed on the floor, he suddenly bends down and snatches up something from behind the chair.*]

AMÉDÉE: A mushroom! Well, really! If they're going to start growing in the dining-room! [*He straightens up and inspects the mushroom*] It's the last straw! ... Poisonous, of course! [*He puts the mushroom down on a corner of the table and gazes at it sourly; he starts pacing about again, becoming more and more agitated, gesticulating and muttering to himself; he glances more*

27

frequently towards the door on the left, goes and writes another word, which he crosses out, then sinks into his armchair. He is worn out.] Oh, that Madeleine, that Madeleine! Once she gets into that bedroom, she's there for ever! [*Plaintively*] She must have seen enough by now! We've both seen enough of him! Oh dear, oh dear, oh dear!

[*He says no more, he's quite overcome. A pause. From the right, on the landing, voices can be heard. It is obviously the concierge and a neighbour talking.*]

THE VOICE OF THE CONCIERGE: So you're back from your holidays, Monsieur Victor!

THE NEIGHBOUR'S VOICE: Yes, Madame Coucou. Just back from the North Pole.

THE VOICE OF THE CONCIERGE: I don't suppose you had it very warm there.

THE NEIGHBOUR'S VOICE: Oh, the weather wasn't too bad. But it's true, for someone like you who comes from the south . . .

THE VOICE OF THE CONCIERGE: I'm no southerner, Monsieur Victor. My grandmother's midwife came from Toulon, but my grandmother's always lived in Lille . . .

[*Suddenly, on the word 'Lille', AMÉDÉE, who can stand it no longer, gets up and moves to the left-hand door, opens it still wider and calls out.*]

AMÉDÉE: Madeleine, for Heaven's sake, Madeleine, what are you doing? Haven't you finished yet? Hurry up!

MADELEINE [*appears. She is the same age as her husband, just as tall or even slightly taller, a hard-looking, rough-tempered woman; she has an old shawl over her head and is wearing a wrapper for the housework; she is rather thin and almost grey. Her husband moves aside fairly quickly to allow her to pass; she leaves the door still half open*]: What's the matter with you now? I can't leave you alone for a second! You needn't think I've been enjoying myself!

AMÉDÉE: Don't spend all your time in his room, then! It's not doing you any good! . . . You've seen quite enough of him. It's too late now.

MADELEINE: I've got to sweep up, haven't I? After all, someone's got to look after the house. We've no maid and there's no one to help me. *And* I've got to earn a living for both of us.

AMÉDÉE: I know. I know we haven't a maid. You never stop reminding me . . .

MADELEINE [*setting to work, sweeping or dusting the room*]: Naturally, no one's even the right to complain where you're concerned . . .

AMÉDÉE: Look here, Madeleine, don't be so unfair . . .

MADELEINE: That's right, go on! Now tell me it's my fault!

AMÉDÉE: You know perfectly well, my dear, that I'm the first to sympathize with you, and what's more I'm the only one; I find the whole situation most unsettling, I blame myself, but . . . I think, after all, you might . . . well, for instance, you take a quarter of an hour to clean out a room this size, and when it comes to his room, which is smaller, a couple of hours is not long enough . . . you hang about in there, just gazing at him . . .

MADELEINE: So now you're timing me! Now I'm supposed to make my lord and master a recital of everything I do, account for every second of my life, I don't belong to myself any more, I'm not myself any more, I'm a slave . . .

AMÉDÉE: Slavery has been abolished, my love . . .

MADELEINE: I'm not your love . . .

AMÉDÉE: Slaves belong to the past . . .

MADELEINE: Well, I'm a modern slave, then!

AMÉDÉE: You don't try to understand. It's just because I'm sorry for you that . . .

MADELEINE: I don't want your pity. Hypocrite! Liar!

AMÉDÉE: You see, it's because I'm really sorry for you that I won't have . . . oh dear . . . that I'd rather you didn't stay in there and watch him. It doesn't do you any good, and it doesn't help . . .

MADELEINE [*indifferently*]: Oh, go and shut the door! Well, what are you waiting for? There's a draught . . .

AMÉDÉE: All the other doors and windows are shut; how can there possibly be a draught?

[*He goes and shuts the left-hand door, after a brief glance into the room which is presumably on the other side;* MADELEINE, *who watches him, does not fail to notice.*]

MADELEINE: What do you think you're doing? Now *you're* looking at him! . . . I get blamed if *I* do it . . . *Will* you shut that door! . . .

AMÉDÉE [*finally closes the door and then comes towards Madeleine*]: I was only looking to see if he'd grown! . . . You'd almost think he had, a little.

MADELEINE [*sharply*]: Not since yesterday . . . or at least not that you'd notice!

AMÉDÉE: It may be all over, you know. Perhaps he's stopped.

MADELEINE: Oh, you and your silly 'look on the bright side'. We know all about *your* forecasts, I'd rather you wrote that play of yours. [*She looks at the table while dusting*] You don't seem to have made much progress. You're still on the first scene. You'll never finish it!

AMÉDÉE: I shall . . . I've added another speech, anyway.

[*He opens the notebook.* MADELEINE *stops working, broom or duster in hand, and listens while he reads*:]

The old man says to the old woman: 'It won't do by itself!'

MADELEINE: Is that all?

AMÉDÉE [*laying the notebook down*]: I've no inspiration. With all I have on my conscience . . . the life we're leading . . . it's not exactly the right atmosphere . . .

MADELEINE: You've never been short of excuses . . .

AMÉDÉE: I feel so tired, so tired . . . worn out, heavy. I've got indigestion and my tummy's all blown out. I feel sleepy all the time.

MADELEINE: Well, you sleep all day!

AMÉDÉE: That's because I'm sleepy.

MADELEINE: I'm tired, too, dog-tired. And *I* go on working, working, working . . .

AMÉDÉE: I can't stick it. Perhaps it's my liver. I feel I've

aged. Of course, I'm not exactly young any more. Still, to
feel like this . . .

MADELEINE: Then rest. What's to stop you resting? Sleep at
night and give up dozing during the day. Stop overeating.
It's all the result of self-indulgence. You drink too much.

AMÉDÉE: *You've* never seen me drunk.

MADELEINE: More than once!

AMÉDÉE: That's not true.

MADELEINE: You don't need to be drunk all the time to
become an alcoholic! . . . It's that little drink before
dinner. That's what gradually poisons your whole
system! . . .

AMÉDÉE: You know I never touch anything but tomato
juice . . .

MADELEINE: Well, then, if you've always been such a sober-
sides, if you've nothing seriously wrong with you, if all your
faculties are still intact, wake yourself up a bit, get to work,
write your masterpiece . . .

AMÉDÉE: I tell you I've no inspiration . . .

MADELEINE: Always the same old story! How do other
people manage, I wonder? It's fifteen years since you had
any inspiration!

AMÉDÉE: Fifteen years. You're right! [*He points to the left-hand
door*] I've not written more than two speeches since he . . .
[*He picks up the notebook and reads*] The old woman says to the
old man, 'Do you think it will do?' and the one I managed
to write today, the one I've just read you: The old man
replies, 'It won't do by itself.' [*He sits down at his table*] I
simply must get down to it. Write, in the state I'm in! A
man should be in a state of elation to do creative work.
You'd need to be a hero, a superman, to write in my
situation, in such wretched poverty . . .

MADELEINE: Have you ever seen a superman living in
poverty? You must be the first!

AMÉDÉE: I must, I *must* get down to it. It's hard, terribly
hard, but I simply *must* get down to it! . . .

[*He has collapsed at his table, leaning on his elbows, his head*

*in his hands, staring vacantly, drawn and haggard; then slowly
his arms fall along the table with his forehead resting on it.
Dumb show. Meanwhile* MADELEINE *has finished her clean-
ing; when she sees her husband's attitude, she shrugs her
shoulders and mutters between her teeth:*]

MADELEINE [*aside*]: Lazy so-and-so!

[*She takes off her apron and her shawl, bundling them up with
her broom and duster, and makes for the left-hand door; as she
reaches it and half opens it,* AMÉDÉE *suddenly raises his
head.*]

AMÉDÉE: Are you going into his room again! . . .

MADELEINE [*showing him what she is carrying*]: I hope you
don't mind if I get rid of all this! Where do you expect me
to put it? I can't leave it all in the dining-room! We haven't
got dozens of rooms, you know!

AMÉDÉE: No, of course not. But don't stay there too long.

MADELEINE: I couldn't in any case. You know perfectly
well I've got to get to work to earn our living . . . And what
a living!

[*She goes into the room on the left.* AMÉDÉE *watches her with
a worried look, hesitates, then gets up and moves cautiously
towards the left-hand door, which has been left half open; he
makes a despondent gesture and suddenly turns to go back to his
table, but he is too late, and* MADELEINE *bumps into him as she
comes back.*]

MADELEINE: Look out, can't you? That hurt!

AMÉDÉE: I'm sorry, I didn't do it on purpose! . . .

MADELEINE: It's really too much! . . . Spying on me now!

AMÉDÉE: Is he still growing?

MADELEINE: Shut the door. Were you born in a barn?

[AMÉDÉE *goes to shut the door, but delays a moment to glance
into the adjoining room.*]

Shut the door, will you!

[AMÉDÉE *pushes the door slowly to, still gazing out until the
last possible moment.*]

Shut it properly!

[AMÉDÉE *does so;* MADELEINE *notices the mushroom*

32

AMÉDÉE *has picked and put down either on a chair or on the corner of the table.*]

Where did you find it?

AMÉDÉE: There, on the floor.

MADELEINE: In the dining-room?

AMÉDÉE: Yes, in the dining-room.

MADELEINE: Why didn't you tell me straightaway? You're always hiding things from me!

AMÉDÉE: I didn't want to upset you . . . You've plenty to worry you as it is.

MADELEINE [*most upset, in a whining voice*]: I don't know – if they're going to start growing in the dining-room now, what's to become of us? All the extra work, too . . . Pulling them up . . . As though I hadn't enough already! . . . Oh dear, oh dear, oh dear!

AMÉDÉE: Sssh! . . . I'll pull them up for you . . . I'll help you . . .

MADELEINE: Oh, I can never rely on you – besides, it's insanitary.

AMÉDÉE: There's only one . . . Just a tiny little one. Perhaps there won't be any more.

MADELEINE: Optimistic as usual, looking on the bright side! I know where that lands us. There's no point in deluding ourselves, we've got to face facts. That's just how it started in *his* room, too. 'Just a tiny little one', you said, 'not to worry, just a freak, an accident.' And *now* . . .

AMÉDÉE: You've found some more today, in the other room?

MADELEINE: You're always wondering why I spend so long in there! I don't go in there for my health!

AMÉDÉE: No, I never said you did . . . But you don't miss a chance to stand and gape at him; you can't take your eyes off him.

MADELEINE: I pulled up fifty only just now.

AMÉDÉE: You see! We're getting the better of them, there were more yesterday.

MADELEINE: Yesterday there were forty-seven . . . *that* was enough.

33

AMÉDÉE [*desperately*]: They're spreading, then, still spreading!

MADELEINE: Everywhere! ... All over the place ... In between the floorboards, round the walls, on the ceiling.

AMÉDÉE [*trying to seek comfort*]: They *are* very tiny. It may have nothing to do with him after all ... Perhaps it's only the damp ... It often happens, you know, in flats. And you never know, they may be good for something: perhaps they keep spiders away ...

MADELEINE: I suppose you've often seen mushrooms growing in flats?

AMÉDÉE: It *does* happen, I promise you. In small provincial towns, especially. Sometimes in the big ones – Lyons, for example.

MADELEINE: I have no idea whether mushrooms sprout in flats in Lyons, but they certainly don't in Paris.

AMÉDÉE: We never go out. We never visit anyone. We've been living shut up here for fifteen years. Perhaps it's different now, in Paris too. Or even in the neighbours' flats. ... Paris mushrooms! ... How can you really be sure!

MADELEINE: Don't talk such nonsense! I'm not a child. It's all because of him. [*With a look and a gesture towards the left-hand door.*] Only because of him.

AMÉDÉE [*resigning himself to the truth, his arms hanging loosely, overcome*]: Yes. Of course, you're right. There can't be any other reason.

MADELEINE: It'll be quite impossible if he makes them grow in here, too. If he's not satisfied with his own room, we won't be able to go on living in this place at all! [*Distraught*] And it wasn't what you'd call cheerful before!

AMÉDÉE: Come on now, Madeleine, pull yourself together! ... Perhaps there won't be any more. We'll see. It may be just a freak, an accident. ...

MADELEINE [*raising her head to look at the clock*]: Nine o'clock! It's time. I must go to work, whatever happens, or I shall be late!

AMÉDÉE: Hurry up, then.

MADELEINE [*as she puts on her hat*]: I shall get into a row.
They'll be starting any moment now . . .
   [*A buzz from the switchboard.*]
They've started already . . . I'm coming . . . [*More gently
to Amédée*] Try and do a little work, too, write
something . . .

AMÉDÉE: I'll try, I promise . . .

MADELEINE [*goes quickly to the switchboard, sits down, picks up
her head-phones, and passes on the call, while* AMÉDÉE *too goes
and sits down at his table with his notebook before him; the clock
advances a quarter of an hour. It is 9.15*]: Hallo? Can I help
you? The President of the Republic? The President in
person or his secretary? . . . Ah, the President . . .

AMÉDÉE [*at his table, re-reading what he has written*]: The old
woman to the old man: 'Do you think it will do?'

MADELEINE [*at the switchboard*]: The President of the
Republic is on tour, Sir, try again in half-an-hour! . . .

AMÉDÉE [*at the table*]: The old man to the old woman . . .

MADELEINE [*at the switchboard; it buzzes again*]: Hallo,
hallo . . .

AMÉDÉE [*at the table, as before*]: . . . The old man to the old
woman . . .

MADELEINE [*as before*]: Mr Charles Chaplin, the grocer?
I'll put you through.
   [*Another buzz.*]
Hallo, hallo . . .

AMÉDÉE [*as before*]: 'It won't do by itself!' . . .

MADELEINE [*as before*]: No, Sir, no. The President can't take
a call for another half hour, I've just told you . . .

AMÉDÉE [*as before*]: . . . The old woman to the old man: 'Do
you think it will do?'

MADELEINE [*as before*]: A call from the King of the Lebanon
. . . [*Another call; she listens in on another line.*] Hold on,
please! [*She plugs in*] Hallo, the Elysée Palace? The
Elysée?!

AMÉDÉE [*as before*]: The old man to the old woman . . .

MADELEINE [*as before*]: Yes, of course there's a King of the
Lebanon ... but I tell you he's on the line! ... Is that the
President? There's a call for you, Sir. [*Another line.*] Go
ahead, please, it's the President of the Republic ...

AMÉDÉE [*as before*]: ... 'No, it won't do by itself.'

MADELEINE [*as before, taking another call. The clock shows
9.30.*]: Hallo, I'm putting you through. [*Another call, another line.*] No, Sir, there are no gas chambers left,
not since the last war ... You'd better wait for the next
one. ...

AMÉDÉE [*still at the table, to Madeleine*]: Madeleine, I can't
think of the next line ...

MADELEINE [*to Amédée*]: Can't you see I'm busy? ...
   [*Buzz*]
   ... Hallo ... I'm sorry, the firemen are away on Thurs-
days, it's their day off, they take the children out for a walk
... But I didn't say today was Thursday.
   [*Another buzz.*]
   Yes ... Hallo ... I'm putting you through ...

AMÉDÉE [*standing up, his hands still on the table*]: Oh, how
tiring it is to write ... I feel worn out! ...

MADELEINE [*as before, answering another call*]: Yes ... you
wish to speak to his wife? ... You don't mind if she takes
it from the bathroom?
   [AMÉDÉE *sits down again heavily.* MADELEINE *goes on as
   before; answering another call, then another, and so on, while
   the clock hands move round to 9.45, and then 10 o'clock*]
   ... I'm putting you through ... I'm putting you
through ...

AMÉDÉE [*with a vacant stare*]: ... the old woman with a
vacant stare ...

MADELEINE [*as before*]: ... Hold on, please, I'm putting
you through ...

AMÉDÉE [*with a sudden glint in his eyes; he's 'found' it*]: ... 'Oh,
yes; it will do all right!' ...

MADELEINE [*as before*]: You're through ...

AMÉDÉE: Madeleine! ... Would you like me to read you

what I've just written? ... You can tell me if it's any good! ...

MADELEINE [*who has lifted her head-phones slightly to hear what* AMÉDÉE *is saying*]: I haven't time just now! ... In a minute! ... [*Another call*]. Hallo ... hold on please ... [*The calls follow in quick succession; the clock hands sweep on; she says*] I'm putting him through ... I'm putting her through ... I'm putting them through ... Hallo, hallo ... hallo ... I'm putting him through ... I'm putting her through ... I'm putting them through ... Hallo ... Hallo! ...

> [AMÉDÉE, *taking advantage of the fact that his wife is fully occupied at the switchboard, gets up quietly, goes towards the left-hand door, looks into the room as he stands in the doorway, turns his head to make sure his wife cannot see what he is doing and then goes softly into the room, leaving the door half open.*
> MADELEINE *is still listening in; another buzz.*]

Hallo, yes, can I help you? ... No, Madame, no, we're a Republic now. ... Since 1870, Madame ... [*Without leaving her place, to Amédée*] Amédée, why is there a draught? ...

> [*Buzz.*]

Yes, I'll put her through ... Amédée, can't you hear me? ... [*She turns her head and notices his absence*] Oh! He's gone into that room again ... What a hopeless, obstinate creature ... [*Just as the clock shows 10.15, she gets up and moves towards the left-hand door, angrily, dragging her feet*] Amédée, do you hear? What are you doing? Messing about in there, instead of writing your play! I'm calling you!

> [*She goes into the room, still leaving the door half open; only their voices can be heard; from time to time there is a short buzz at the switchboard, not too loud and left unanswered.*]

MADELEINE [*from the room, in the wings to the left*]: You were watching him ...

AMÉDÉE: I couldn't help myself ...

MADELEINE: It won't do any good, it won't *help*.

AMÉDÉE: Suddenly I began to hope . . . I wondered if . . . I thought he might have disappeared. . . .

MADELEINE: Just like that, all by himself! You're out of your mind!

AMÉDÉE: The day of miracles is past . . . unfortunately . . .

MADELEINE: Come along now . . . come *along*!

[MADELEINE *comes out of the left-hand room, dragging Amédée behind her.*]

AMÉDÉE: I feel quite sick! . . . Every time I look at him.

MADELEINE: Don't look, then! What did you go to his room for?

AMÉDÉE: I feel quite sick . . .

MADELEINE: Any excuse to stop writing . . .

AMÉDÉE: He's grown again. Soon, the divan won't be big enough for him. His feet are over the end already. I seem to remember fifteen years ago he was rather short. And so young. Now he's got a great white beard. He's quite imposing with that white beard. Twenty and fifteen, that only makes him thirty-five, after all. . . . He's not really old . . .

MADELEINE: The dead grow old faster than the living. Everyone knows that . . .

[AMÉDÉE, *quite overcome, goes and collapses into the armchair;* MADELEINE *is in the centre of the stage.*]

AMÉDÉE: Oh! What big nails he's got!

MADELEINE: I can't cut them every day. I've got other things to do! Last week I threw a whole handful into the dustbin . . . It's not easy to do either. I'm just a servant, I am, just a drudge, waiting on everyone.

AMÉDÉE: His toenails have grown right through his shoes . . .

MADELEINE: Then buy him another pair, if you've got money to burn! What do you expect *me* to do? I'm not giving you any! We're very poor! You don't seem to realize!

AMÉDÉE: Well, I can't very well give him mine, can I?

They're my only pair. Besides, they'd never fit him . . .
Now his feet have got so large!

[*Buzz;* MADELEINE *goes quickly to the switchboard.*]

MADELEINE: Hallo, yes? Can I help you? . . .

[*Meanwhile* AMÉDÉE *gets up from his armchair, goes once
more towards the half-open door on the left, and stares out
petrified.*]

. . . No, Sir, he's not there . . . At least, I shouldn't think
so.

AMÉDÉE [*without moving*]: The shutters are fastened tight.
Yet it's not dark in his room.

MADELEINE [*moves up to Amédée; each time she leaves her
office, she takes off her hat; she puts it on again whenever she goes
back*]: The light comes from his eyes. You've forgotten to
close the lids again.

AMÉDÉE: His eyes haven't aged. They're still as beautiful.
Great green eyes. Shining like beacons. I'd better go and
close them for him.

MADELEINE: And *you* think they're beautiful! You're talking
like a book. You've plenty of inspiration in real life. Funny
idea of beauty, though.

AMÉDÉE: I didn't say it was funny.

MADELEINE: We could get along without his kind of beauty,
it takes up too much space.

[*Slight cracking noises can be heard coming from the adjoining
room.*]

Did you hear that?

AMÉDÉE: He's growing. It's quite natural. He's branching
out.

MADELEINE: What do you take him for, a tree? He's just
making himself at home! Why, he'll soon monopolize the
whole place! Where am I going to put him? *You* don't
care. *You* don't have to do the housework!

AMÉDÉE: Of course, I know, he gives us a lot of trouble, but
in spite of that he's made a great impression on me. When I
think . . . ah, it might all have been so different . . .

MADELEINE: Now I suppose you're going to find another

excuse to stand there doing nothing . . . Go and write!

AMÉDÉE: All right! . . . All right! . . .

[*Buzz*]

MADELEINE [*while* AMÉDÉE *makes for his desk-table*]: Never a minute's peace! [*Picking up the head-phones, to Amédée*] Shut the door! [*Answering the telephone*] Hallo, yes, can I help you? . . .

AMÉDÉE [*returns to the door, puts his hand on the door-knob, looks again into the room, glances at Madeleine busy at the switchboard and seems to hesitate; then he closes the door and returns again to his table to work. He sits down*]: The old man says to the old woman . . .

[*Another buzz*].

MADELEINE [*to Amédée, before answering the telephone*]: You still haven't closed the lids! [*At the telephone*] Yes, Your Worship the Mayor? I'll put you through to the Mayoress.

AMÉDÉE: I'm going . . .

[*He gets up and goes towards the door on the left; before he reaches it,* MADELEINE *says:*]

MADELEINE [*to Amédée. The clock should now show 11.15.*]: You might go and do the shopping, or we shan't have anything for lunch. Take the basket.

AMÉDÉE [*annoyed*]: In such circumstances it's not easy to write. And you're surprised I can't get on with it. Afterwards you'll say it's my fault again. I can't work, I can't work! I don't have the normal conditions necessary for intellectual work . . .

MADELEINE: What have you been dreaming about until now? You always seem to discover the will to work at the last minute.

AMÉDÉE: That's not true! . . .

MADELEINE: *I* can't leave my office *either*. You can see that for yourself. I can't risk losing my job, unless you find some other way of supporting us. You don't think I enjoy this, do you? Of course, if you want us both to starve, it's all the same to me.

AMÉDÉE: And it's all the same to me, too. This life's not worth living!

MADELEINE: I don't know what you'd do, if you didn't get enough to eat. You're always complaining you're ravenous, wanting to stuff yourself all day long . . .
[*Buzz.*]
Do you hear what I say? [*She answers the telephone*] Can I help you, Madame! [*To Amédée*] Hurry up and take the basket or there'll be nothing left at the market!
[AMÉDÉE *makes for the left hand-door and lays his hand on the doorknob.*]

MADELEINE [*still at the switchboard, watches him*]: What are you going into his room for now?

AMÉDÉE: The basket . . . the basket . . . You told me to take the basket!

MADELEINE: That's not where it's kept! You never know where anything is!
[*Buzz.*]
Hallo . . . one moment, please! [*To Amédée*] There under the table . . . That's where it's kept. Try not to forget next time. [*On the telephone*] Number engaged!

AMÉDÉE [*bends down and sees the basket*]: Oh yes! . . . And the rope?

MADELEINE: In the basket. [*On the telephone*] Yes, Mademoiselle, of course I'll read you the official statement . . . It's a pleasure.

AMÉDÉE [*picks up the basket and stands up straight*]: Oh yes, this is it.

MADELEINE [*on the telephone*]: It is forbidden for trucks weighing more than ten tons . . . You can take it at dictation speed? Very well, Mademoiselle. Yes, I'll read it slowly. No trouble at all . . . Take your time, I'm in no hurry . . .

AMÉDÉE [*walks very slowly to the rear window, holding the basket, which has a rope tied to the handle; the hands of the clock should now stand at 11.45*]: This rope isn't very long. It's a good thing we only live on the first floor.

MADELEINE [*at the telephone*]: It is forbidden for trucks weighing more than ten tons . . . That's right, ten tons . . . to cross the permanent way . . .

[AMÉDÉE *gently raises the Venetian blinds, or pushes the shutters a short way and, holding the rope, lowers the basket.*] Amédée, what are you doing? People will see us!

AMÉDÉE [*his head turned towards Madeleine*]: I've got to lower the basket! . . .

MADELEINE [*at the telephone*]: No . . . I was speaking to my husband, I'm so sorry . . . [*To Amédée*] Don't buy any sausages, pork upsets you. [*At the telephone*] . . . to cross the permanent way between midnight and eight o'clock in the morning . . .

AMÉDÉE [*to Madeleine*]: What must I buy then?

MADELEINE [*to Amédée*]: Buy what you like. [*At the telephone*] . . . without written authority . . .

AMÉDÉE [*addressing someone presumably down below in the street*]: Put in a pound of plums, please! . . . A cream cheese.

MADELEINE [*at the telephone*]: . . . without written authority from the Sanitary Inspector . . .

AMÉDÉE [*as before*]: . . . Two rusks, two pots of yoghourt . . .

MADELEINE [*at the telephone*]: . . . which may be obtained on submission of a written request to Police Headquarters . . .

AMÉDÉE [*as before*]: . . . fifty grammes of table salt . . .

MADELEINE [*as before*]: . . . countersigned by the Chief Constable.

AMÉDÉE [*as before*]: . . . That's all . . . Thank you . . . You can let go. [*He pulls the basket up by the rope.*]

MADELEINE [*as before*]: Hallo . . . Yes, that's right, Mademoiselle . . . Oh, no . . . You needn't read it back . . . Thanks all the same.

[AMÉDÉE *has pulled the basket in and closed the shutters; he goes and empties the contents of the basket out on the table, next to his notebooks. It is noon by the clock.*]

MADELEINE: Twelve o'clock. [*She lays the head-phones down*] At last! . . . [*She takes off her hat and goes towards Amédée.*]

AMÉDÉE: Have you finished?

MADELEINE: Yes and about time too. I'm exhausted . . . I don't like this brand of cream cheese. You've forgotten the leeks.

AMÉDÉE: You didn't tell me to buy any. [*Nodding his head towards the left-hand door*] I say, Madeleine, do you think he's forgiven us?

MADELEINE [*sitting down to table facing the door on the left, while* AMÉDÉE *is still standing facing the same way*]: I don't know.

AMÉDÉE: We can't tell. [*He makes a move towards the door.*]

MADELEINE: Sit down and eat. What are you waiting for?

AMÉDÉE [*sitting down next to Madeleine, but facing the audience*]: He may have forgiven us. I believe he has.

[*A long heavy silence; they are eating their plums.*]
Ah, if only we could be sure he'd forgiven us!
[*Another silence.*]

MADELEINE: If he'd forgiven us, he'd have stopped growing. As he's still growing, he must still be feeling spiteful. He still has a grudge against us. The dead are terribly vindictive. The living forget much sooner.

AMÉDÉE: Dash it! They've got their whole lives in front of them! . . . Perhaps he's not as wicked as the others. He wasn't very wicked when he was alive . . .

MADELEINE: That's what you think! They're all alike. Look, I tell you he's growing. He's sowing mushrooms all over the place. If that isn't wickedness!

AMÉDÉE: Perhaps he's not doing it on purpose! He's growing very slowly . . . only a little at a time.

MADELEINE: A bit more every day, every day a bit more, it all adds up . . .
[*Silence.*]

AMÉDÉE: Do you mind if I go and look? Perhaps he's stopped.

MADELEINE: I will not have him talked about at table.

AMÉDÉE: Don't upset yourself, Madeleine . . .

MADELEINE: I want to have my lunch in peace. At least, let's have peace and quiet at meal-times. I've worries enough all day. I'm not asking too much, I hope! . . .

AMÉDÉE: No, Madeleine. Just as you like, Madeleine.
[*They eat in silence.*]

MADELEINE: It's so hot in here. I'm stifling . . .

AMÉDÉE: I hadn't noticed it.

MADELEINE: Open the door, and let's have a little air . . .

AMÉDÉE: Which door?

MADELEINE [*indicating the left-hand door*]: That one. You surely weren't thinking of opening the landing door.

AMÉDÉE: You're getting excited again.

MADELEINE: It's not that I want to look at him, I tell you. I'm too hot. I want a breath of air, that's all.

AMÉDÉE: Now listen, Madeleine . . . It's not very wise.

MADELEINE: Please do as I ask.

AMÉDÉE: Very well . . . But I think it's a mistake . . . [*He gets up, opens the door, and returns to the table.*] It won't make it any cooler, you know. There won't be any more air. The windows in his room are closed.

[MADELEINE *is gazing through the open door from where she is sitting; she has stopped eating.*]

Aren't you hungry?

[MADELEINE *does not reply.*]

Aren't you hungry?

MADELEINE: Oh, leave me alone, give me a moment to breathe . . .

[*The eyes of both are fixed on the room. A short silence.*] What have I ever done to deserve this . . . to be persecuted like this . . .

AMÉDÉE: It's just the same for me, you know . . .

MADELEINE: No, it's not. You don't feel it so much, you're not so sensitive.

AMÉDÉE: Well, I . . .

MADELEINE: I didn't mean it that way. I'm not blaming you. You're just luckier than I am.

AMÉDÉE: Luckier than you?

MADELEINE: Of course. At least you can write and think about something else, with all your books and literature, you can escape from the worry of it . . . whereas I've got nothing . . . Nothing but the office and the housework . . .

AMÉDÉE: Poor Madeleine!

MADELEINE [*annoyed*]: I don't need your pity either . . .
[*A short silence; they look towards the room.*]

AMÉDÉE: You'd almost think he was breathing. [*A short silence.*] What an expressive face he's got! [*Silence.*] You'd almost think he could hear us.

MADELEINE: Well, we're not saying anything bad about him!
[*Silence.*]

AMÉDÉE: He *is* handsome.

MADELEINE: He *was* handsome. He's too old now.

AMÉDÉE: He's *still* handsome! . . . [*Silence.*] Has he forgiven us yet? Has he forgiven us? [*Short pause.*] We put him in the best room, *our* bedroom when we were first married . . .
[*He tries to take Madeleine's hand, but she withdraws it.*]

MADELEINE: Finish your lunch! Brrr! . . . I feel terribly cold . . .

AMÉDÉE: Would you like me to shut the door?

MADELEINE [*not listening to him*]: Bring me my shawl.

AMÉDÉE [*rises slowly to his feet, stands and glances for a moment into the room, then goes to look for Madeleine's shawl in some other part of the dining-room, and says*]: You'd almost believe he could see us!

MADELEINE: You've forgotten to close the lids again! You see, you never remember! It's always, always left to me!

AMÉDÉE: Yes . . . I'll go and fetch your shawl first, you're cold! . . .

MADELEINE: I'd rather you closed his eyelids!
[AMÉDÉE *makes for the left-hand room: steps are heard on the stairs; then a cough.*]

AMÉDÉE [*stopping within a yard of the bedroom door*]: Ssh! Someone's coming.

MADELEINE: Well, who do you think it is? It's one of the neighbours coming home. No one has been to see us for fifteen years! We've lost touch with everybody.

AMÉDÉE: One visit would be enough.

[*A voice is heard on the landing.*]

Listen!

[*Someone can be vaguely heard saying 'Buccinioni'.*]

I heard them say our name.

MADELEINE: [*becoming alarmed*]: You're imagining things!
[*However, the name 'Buccinioni' is heard again, more distinctly this time:* MADELEINE *rises.*]

Good Heavens! . . . [*To Amédée*] What did I tell you?
[*They both listen breathlessly while the following is heard:*]

THE POSTMAN'S VOICE [*on the landing*]: M. Buccinioni's flat please?

THE VOICE OF THE CONCIERGE [*on the landing*]: It's right opposite. They're sure to be in. They never go out.
[*Noise of a door being shut.*]

MADELEINE [*to Amédée*]: I told you it was for us . . . Oh dear, oh dear!

AMÉDÉE [*losing his head*]: We mustn't lose our heads . . .
[*A knock is heard on the right.*]

MADELEINE [*indicating the left-hand door*]: For Heaven's sake shut that door!
[AMÉDÉE *hurriedly pushes the door to, while* MADELEINE *dashes over to it and stands with her back to it as though at bay; she is panic-stricken: more knocking at the door on the right. Her hand on her heart:*]

Go and see . . .

[AMÉDÉE *hesitates.*]

Go and see. It doesn't help not to answer. It would only make things worse. It's so easy to break a door in.
[AMÉDÉE *makes for the right-hand door, while the following is heard from the landing:*]

THE VOICE OF THE CONCIERGE: Knock a little louder! They're always at home!
[*Several knocks.*]

MADELEINE [*without moving, in a whisper*]: Open it, go on . . .
[AMÉDÉE *moves to do so.*] No, don't . . .

AMÉDÉE [*to Madeleine*]: It wouldn't do any good. It's so easy to break a door in.

MADELEINE: Have a peep and see who it is, first.

AMÉDÉE [*to Madeleine*]: Ssh! [*Then he bends down cautiously and looks through the keyhole, while the following is heard from the landing.*]

THE VOICE OF THE CONCIERGE: Knock louder, they can't have heard you.

[*This makes* MADELEINE *and* AMÉDÉE *jump violently.*]

MADELEINE [*with a beating heart*]: Oh my God! Who on earth can it be? We don't know anybody . . .

AMÉDÉE [*straightening up, to Madeleine*]: The postman!

THE POSTMAN [*from outside*]: M. Buccinioni! M. Buccinioni!

MADELEINE [*terrified*]: A postman! Impossible! You've made a mistake . . . It's all your fault, you and your old friends, it's all because of your old friends . . .

AMÉDÉE [*while* MADELEINE *stands there gasping, with out-stretched arms, as though ready to forbid anyone to enter the room*]: I'm just coming! I'll open the door, why shouldn't I open it?

[*He opens the door. The* POSTMAN *comes in.*]

You see, you can come in, now I've opened the door, come right in, I've nothing to hide, there's nothing to hide in this flat.

MADELEINE [*almost clinging to the door-frame*]: We've nothing to hide, there's nothing to hide in this flat.

AMÉDÉE: My wife and I were just saying: 'Why shouldn't we open the door?'

THE POSTMAN [*as though there was nothing unusual*]: Perfectly natural, Sir.

MADELEINE [*without moving, to Amédée*]: Why does he say it's natural? [*To the Postman*] Why do you say it's natural?

THE POSTMAN [*still quite indifferent*]: A letter for you . . .

AMÉDÉE: Oh no, there can't be.

MADELEINE: Who'd write to us? That's just what I was saying to my husband! Are you really only a postman?

AMÉDÉE [*to Madeleine*]: Of course he is, Madeleine. What *are* you thinking of?

MADELEINE [*to the Postman*]: Then you can't possibly have a

47

letter for us! Who do you think we are for people to write to us?

THE POSTMAN: Yes, a letter for M. Amédée Buccinioni!

MADELEINE: That's our name! [*She has come slightly away from the door, but returns quickly as soon as she realizes it*] There's nothing, nobody in this room!

AMÉDÉE [*taking the letter from the Postman*]: Why, yes he's right! It's amazing, but it is for us: Amédée Buccinioni . . .

MADELEINE: How awful!

[*The* POSTMAN *turns to go, while* AMÉDÉE *is examining the letter.*]

AMÉDÉE: Look! It's a mistake, it really is a mistake!

THE POSTMAN: You're not M. Amédée Buccinioni, then?

AMÉDÉE: I'm not the only Amédée Buccinioni in Paris! Nearly half the people in Paris have that name.

[*He holds out the letter to the* POSTMAN, *who takes it back. A prolonged cracking noise comes from the room on the left.* MADELEINE, *horrified, stifles a scream, then utters a peal of laughter to cover the noise.*]

THE POSTMAN: Yet I take it you are M. Amédée Buccinioni of number twenty-nine, Generals Road . . .

AMÉDÉE: There's more than one number twenty-nine, Generals Road, there's more than one Generals Road, there are lots of them . . . [*He casts a worried look at the floor, just by the table, and shows something to Madeleine, who is still motionless.*] . . . Another one, Madeleine! . . . generals sprout like mushrooms . . .

THE POSTMAN [*poker-faced*]: You grow house mushrooms?

AMÉDÉE [*quickly, to the Postman*]: You see, it really is a mistake. I am not Amédée Buccinioni, but A-MÉ-DÉE-BUCCINIONI; I don't live at twenty-nine Generals Road, but at twenty-nine Generals Road . . . You see, the capital A of Amédée on the envelope is written in round hand; my Christian name, Amédée, begins with a Roman capital . . .

MADELEINE: They insisted on calling him after his god-father! You see, it *was* a mistake.

THE POSTMAN [*examining the letter*]: You're right, Monsieur, what you say is correct.

AMÉDÉE [*to the Postman*]: Nobody knows us at all, nobody ever writes to us, I assure you.

THE POSTMAN: Sorry to have troubled you. Sign, please, Monsieur! [*He presents a notebook.*]

MADELEINE: You're not going to make us sign that, are you? We're respectable people.

THE POSTMAN: Oh, it doesn't matter, Madame. It's optional. So sorry. Good day to you! [*He turns to go.*]

MADELEINE: *We're* sorry we can't offer you a glass of wine. We've nothing in the flat; you see, my husband doesn't drink.

AMÉDÉE [*to the Postman*]: It's quite true. I don't drink. It doesn't agree with me.

MADELEINE: We're really very sorry.

THE POSTMAN: That's all right. It's not the custom in Paris. It's only country postmen who get a glass of wine. [*He leaves.*]
[AMÉDÉE *hurries forward to open the door for him.*]

AMÉDÉE: Good-bye! [*He closes the door, glances for a moment through the keyhole, then straightens up briskly.*] Phew! . . . It wasn't for us after all! Do you think he was annoyed?

MADELEINE [*coming to the centre of the stage, complaining*]: No one ever writes to us! Not a single soul! We haven't a friend left! We broke with everyone, absolutely everyone! We couldn't invite them home.

AMÉDÉE [*looking about everywhere on the floor for the mushroom*]: I could have sworn I saw one just now!

MADELEINE [*pointing to the room and finishing her sentence*]: . . . with *him* here . . .

AMÉDÉE [*going down on his knees, then getting up again, a mushroom in his hand*]: Here it is! I've found it!

MADELEINE: The second one in the dining-room . . . Don't put it on the table, silly, it's not sanitary, and you know they're poisonous. [*A short silence.*] Listen, today I'll let you break your rule. Have a glass of wine, go on, you look so miserable!

[*A tremendous crack is suddenly heard from the adjoining room.*]
Oh! I'm frightened!

AMÉDÉE: It's only him, Madeleine, don't be afraid!

[*A loud crash of breaking glass from the same direction;*
AMÉDÉE *rushes to the door, followed by* MADELEINE.]

MADELEINE: Don't stand there like that! Go and see!

AMÉDÉE: What can have happened now! [*They both disappear through the door, which they leave wide open; coming from the wings, left*] He's smashed the window! . . . His head's gone right through!

MADELEINE [*in the wings*]: He's growing both ends at once! What's he up to now! *Do* something, Amédée. The neighbours will see him! Pull his head in!

AMÉDÉE [*in the wings*]: That's what I *am* doing!

MADELEINE [*her back framed in the door*]: Hurry up!
[*A dull thud.*]
Don't drag his head on the floor! You are a clumsy devil!

AMÉDÉE [*in the wings*]: It's not so easy!

MADELEINE: Lift him up. Lay his head on the cushion. Don't forget to close his eyes!

AMÉDÉE [*in the wings*]: I can't. There's not enough room.

MADELEINE [*still framed in the doorway*]: Well, fold him in two then, fold him in two, it's easy enough!
[AMÉDÉE *can be heard breathing heavily with the effort.*]
No, not like that. [MADELEINE *goes back into the room and can be heard saying*] Let *me* do it!
[AMÉDÉE'*s back now appears, framed in the doorway. From the wings:*]
That's it. Like this. I have to show you everything!

AMÉDÉE [*still in the doorway*]: I was doing my best . . . You're never satisfied . . . Are the neighbours looking out of their windows?

MADELEINE [*from the wings*]: No . . . Come and help me. You always leave me to do the hardest part by myself.

AMÉDÉE [*disappears once more into the room; he leaves the door wide open and can be heard saying*]: But I thought you wanted . . .

MADELEINE [*louder, but still off-stage*]: Now pull, pull harder!
 [*Their efforts are clearly audible; a dull thud.*]
 Look out! Be careful!
 [*More noise.*]
 Close the shutters properly! It'll be cold in here now, with-
 out the glass!

AMÉDÉE: It's not nearly winter yet.
 [AMÉDÉE *and* MADELEINE *reappear.*]

MADELEINE: That's that!

AMÉDÉE: You see, it's all right in the end.

MADELEINE [*changes her mind as she is about to shut the door*]:
 Go and close his eyes! You've forgotten again!
 [AMÉDÉE *starts walking towards the room.*]
 The neighbours must have heard.

AMÉDÉE [*stopping*]: They *may* not have done. [*Short silence.*]
 There's not a sound from them! . . . Besides, at this time of
 day . . .

MADELEINE: They must have heard sòmething. They're not
 all deaf.

AMÉDÉE: Not *all* of them, they couldn't be. But as I say, at
 this time of day . . .

MADELEINE: What could we tell them?

AMÉDÉE: We could say it was the postman!

MADELEINE [*turning her back to the audience and looking towards
 the rear window*]: It was the postman who did it! It was the
 p-o-stman! [*To Amédée*] Will they believe us? The postman
 must have gone, by now.

AMÉDÉE: All the better. [*Loudly shouting to the rear of the stage*]
 It was the p-o-stman!

MADELEINE:
AMÉDÉE: } It was the p-o-stman! The p-o-stman!
 [*They stop shouting, and the echo is heard.*]

ECHO: The p-o-stman! The p-o-stman! P-o-stman! O-o-st-
 man!

AMÉDÉE [*he and* MADELEINE *both turning to face the audience*]:
 You see, even the echo's repeating it.

MADELEINE: Perhaps it isn't the echo!

AMÉDÉE: It strengthens our case, anyhow. It's an alibi!...
Let's sit down.

MADELEINE [*sitting down*]: Life's really getting impossible.
Where are we to find new window-panes?

[*Suddenly, from the adjoining room, a violent bang is heard
against the wall;* AMÉDÉE, *who was about to sit down, stands
up again, his gaze riveted on the left of the stage;* MADELEINE
does the same.]

MADELEINE [*uttering a cry*]: Ah!

AMÉDÉE [*distractedly*]: Keep calm, keep calm!

[*The left-hand door gradually gives way, as though under
steady pressure.*]

MADELEINE [*not far from fainting, but still standing, cries out
again*]: Ah! Heaven help us!

[*Then* AMÉDÉE *and* MADELEINE, *dumb with terror, watch
two enormous feet slide slowly in through the open door and
advance about eighteen inches on to the stage.*]

MADELEINE: Look!

[*This is naturally an anguished cry, yet there should be a certain
restraint about it; it should, of course, convey fear, but above all
irritation. This is an embarrassing situation, but it should not
seem at all unusual, and the actors should play this scene quite
naturally. It is a 'nasty blow' of course, an extremely 'nasty
blow', but no worse than that.*]

AMÉDÉE: I'm looking. [*He rushes forward, lifts the feet and sets
them carefully on a stool or chair.*] Well, that's the limit!

MADELEINE: What's he doing to us now? What does he
want!

AMÉDÉE: He's growing faster and faster!

MADELEINE: Do something, can't you!

AMÉDÉE [*appalled, desperately*]: There's nothing to be done,
nothing. There's nothing left for us to do, I'm afraid! He's
got geometrical progression.

MADELEINE: Geometrical progression!?

AMÉDÉE [*as before*]: Yes ... the incurable disease of the
dead! How could he have caught it here with us!

MADELEINE [*losing control*]: But what's to become of us!

Good God, what's to become of us! I told you this would happen . . . I was sure of it . . .

AMÉDÉE: I'll go and fold him up . . .

MADELEINE: You've done that already!

AMÉDÉE: I'll go and roll him up . . .

MADELEINE: That won't stop him getting bigger. He's growing in all directions at once! Where are we going to put him? What are we to do with him? What's to become of us! [*She buries her head in her hands and weeps.*]

AMÉDÉE: Come on, Madeleine, cheer up!

MADELEINE: Oh no! It's too much, it's more than anyone could stand . . .

AMÉDÉE [*trying to comfort her*]: Everyone has problems, Madeleine.

MADELEINE [*wringing her hands*]: I don't call this living! No, no, it's unbearable.

AMÉDÉE: Think of my parents, for example, they had . . .

MADELEINE [*in tears, interrupting him*]: And now he's going to bring all his mushrooms in here. You've found two already, that was a warning. I should have realized . . .

[*More cracking noises from the adjoining room.*]

AMÉDÉE [*as before*]: Some people are worse off than we are!

MADELEINE [*sobbing, tears, despair*]: You don't understand that it's not natural, it's inhuman, that's what it is, inhuman, completely inhuman! [*She collapses on a chair and sobs, her head in her hands; every now and again she groans.*] It's inhuman, that's what it is, inhuman . . . inhuman . . . inhuman . . .

AMÉDÉE [*has been standing by impotently all this time, his arms hanging at his sides, now looking at Madeleine and taking a step nearer as though to console her, then giving up and gazing at the dead man as he mops his brow; he says to himself*]: What about my plays? I shan't be able to write any now . . . We're finished . . .

[*The feet advance another twelve inches and make* MADELEINE *jump.*]

MADELEINE: Again! [*She buries her face in her hands once more, sobbing and groaning*] . . . inhuman . . . inhuman . . .

AMÉDÉE: Now I shall never be able to . . . We shan't even be able to breathe in this atmosphere!

MADELEINE [*still in the same state and muttering to herself*]: . . . inhuman . . . inhuman . . . [*Then she changes the refrain with*] It's an ideal excuse for you to stop work altogether! [*And returns to*] . . . that's what it is . . . it's inhuman . . .

[*A buzz at the switchboard; she makes a desperate effort to stand up; it is now one o'clock.*]

MADELEINE: Still, it's time for *me* to get back to work again. It's more than I can . . . [*However, she tries to put on her hat and shouts at the switchboard*] All right, I'm coming . . .

AMÉDÉE: Don't go, Madeleine, not today anyhow, you're too tired, rest a little . . .

MADELEINE: I must go. What do you think we're going to live on? We haven't a penny . . .

[*The buzzer goes again, more impatiently.*]

Whatever happens, I've got to . . . [*To the switchboard*] Yes, yes! All right! . . . [*To Amédée*] Other people don't care . . . they only want to squeeze you till the last drop of blood . . . they never think you might be at your last . . . gasp . . . [*Buzz.*]

AMÉDÉE: We've still got some food in reserve, Madeleine! Macaroni, mustard, vinegar, celery . . .

MADELEINE [*collapsing completely*]: We shall go a long way on that . . . I don't care, I can't stand any more, it's too much . . . [*Taking off the hat she has just clamped on anyhow, she hurls it away from her and shouts at the switchboard*] I won't answer. I've had enough . . .

[*The buzzers suddenly stop.*]

. . . more than I can bear . . . [*She falls on a chair; her hat is lying somewhere on the floor; her head is in her hands again and she is sobbing hopelessly.*]

AMÉDÉE [*looks at her and then, completely at a loss, picks her hat up mechanically; he stands there, in the centre of the stage, holding the hat and staring into space; with some violent cracking noises still coming from the adjoining room, he walks very slowly to his arm-*

chair and sinks down in it, all hunched up; in a very tired voice he says]: I can't understand how we ever got into such a mess. It's so unfair . . . And in a case like this . . . no one to turn to for help and advice! . . .

CURTAIN

ACT TWO

The scene is the same. When the act opens it is three o'clock. In the right half of the stage there is more furniture than there was before. It has been brought from the left-hand room, because the dead man has taken up all the space. It includes a divan bed, near the door, right, and perhaps an additional armchair, a bedside table, a standing wash-basin, a mirror, a wardrobe – various bedroom furniture, in fact. These objects are all jumbled round the right-hand door, which is blocked up. The left-hand side of the stage is devoid of furniture, except for a few stools, spaced out so that the feet and legs of the dead man many rest on them; the body takes up a great part of this side of the stage. Also on the left-hand side there are a number of giant mushrooms growing at the foot of the walls. Every now and again the dead man's feet jerk forward towards the right, giving Amédée and Madeleine a violent shock on each occasion. Every time this happens AMÉDÉE *measures the fresh ground covered, automatically, as though it were a reflex action.*

[*As the curtain rises* AMÉDÉE *and* MADELEINE *are on the left of the stage. They are barely visible, concealed by the lumber. Neither of them speaks for a moment, then the dead man's feet suddenly slide forward to the right. At once* MADELEINE'S *head appears, only to disappear again a moment later among the furniture.* AMÉDÉE *comes into the open stage.*]

MADELEINE [*making a brief appearance*]: You can actually *see* him growing.

AMÉDÉE [*goes and makes a chalk mark on the floor by the stool on*

55

which the dead man's feet are resting, and then carefully measures the distance between the old mark and the new one; when he has done this, he says]: Six inches in twenty minutes. He's growing faster than ever . . . Oh dear oh dear! [*For a moment he gazes at the part of the body that is on the stage, then at the enormous mushrooms.*] They're still getting bigger too! [*A silence.*] If they weren't the poisonous variety, we could eat them, or sell them! Oh! I'm really no good at anything: whatever I try! I can never make a go of it.

MADELEINE [*emerging from the lumber and combing her hair in front of the mirror*]: I've been telling you that for ages . . .

AMÉDÉE [*with a sigh*]: Yes, Madeleine, you're right. Anyone else could manage better than I do. I'm like a helpless child, I'm defenceless. I'm a misfit . . . I wasn't made to live in the twentieth century.

MADELEINE: You should have been born earlier . . . or a darn sight later!

[*Silence. With his hands behind his back, rather round-shouldered, he strolls meditatively round the left-hand part of the stage; then he stops.*]

AMÉDÉE: If only my morale was a little higher. It's being so tired. Yet I don't do anything special . . . [*He starts making for the bed on the right and brushes against the dead man's legs*] Oh, I'm so sorry . . .

[*He gently re-arranges the legs and glances at Madeleine to see if she has noticed or not; as he sees she is still busy with her hair, he looks a little more relieved; then, after a few more paces, he suddenly stops. He has an idea. He glances again at Madeleine, then towards the open door to the left, then again at Madeleine; once more towards the door. He has made up his mind; he tiptoes quietly towards the next room and has just reached the doorway when:*]

MADELEINE [*coming right forward into the front of the stage*]: Amédée, where are you going?

[AMÉDÉE *stands stock still.*]

Can't you hear me, Amédée? I want to know where you're going?

AMÉDÉE: Nowhere, nowhere at all ... where could I be going?

MADELEINE: I'm coming with you.

AMÉDÉE: I can't move an inch without you following me! I'm a free man, aren't I?

MADELEINE [*annoyed*]: Do as you please, my dear, go ahead, go ahead if you like ... If you always want to be by yourself! ... If only getting your own way got you somewhere!

AMÉDÉE [*retracing his steps*]: Very well. I'll never go in again, so there! Now are you satisfied?

MADELEINE [*shrugging her shoulders*]: What a nasty temper! You *are* an impossible creature! I need all my patience, with you ... you haven't a single saving grace. You can see where it's got us, you can see the mess we're in ...

AMÉDÉE: Finding fault, always finding fault! When a thing's done, it's done, no use crying over ...

MADELEINE: It's easy to talk! Just to shake off your responsibilities.

AMÉDÉE: It's not altogether *my* fault ...

MADELEINE: Well, I like that! Surely you're not suggesting it's mine! [*She makes for the left-hand room.*]

AMÉDÉE: Where are you going?

MADELEINE: I can't leave him as he is! Someone's got to clean him up, and I can't see you doing it!

AMÉDÉE: Why bother! What's the good!

MADELEINE [*does not in fact go; the dead man's feet advance again*]: He's growing! Growing again!

[AMÉDÉE *moves towards the bed.*]

What are you doing? You still haven't closed his eyes! You've got a memory like a sieve!

AMÉDÉE: I feel so *tired*! [*He goes and collapses on the bed.*]

MADELEINE: As usual, when it's time for you to *do* something! ... Are you going to get rid of him? If you're really so tired, take some medicine, take a tonic ... take *something*.

AMÉDÉE: They have no effect on me any more. They just make me more tired.

MADELEINE: This is a fine time . . .

AMÉDÉE: I've no strength left, no will-power.

MADELEINE: A fine time to give in! At the critical moment your energy always deserts you and your will-power dwindles away. You'll never change, my lad! Will you get rid of him or not?

AMÉDÉE: It'll be all right, it really will, it'll be all right . . . I'm sure it will . . . it's simply got to be all right . . .

MADELEINE: You really believe that, do you? [*Then, suddenly changing her tone*] It's sheer madness! Do you expect it to put itself right? . . . Something has got to be done, something positive! Now listen to me! If you don't get rid of him, I'm going to get a divorce.

AMÉDÉE: It's not the right time to do that. I couldn't look after him all by myself.

MADELEINE: Do you intend to get rid of him, then? Yes or No? Answer me!

AMÉDÉE: I'm thinking about it, Madeleine. Seriously I am.

MADELEINE: You're thinking! It's ages since you first started thinking about it! If you don't decide what to do, the neighbours are bound to notice something. And soon there won't be enough room for him . . .

AMÉDÉE: As if the neighbours cared . . .

MADELEINE: That's what you think. Listen! . . .

[*From the landing can be heard the voice of the* CONCIERGE *and a man's voice.*]

THE VOICE OF THE CONCIERGE: There's something very peculiar going on in this house . . .

THE MAN'S VOICE: Yes, they're a rum lot!

MADELEINE: Did you hear? And it's not the first time I've heard remarks like that . . .

AMÉDÉE: Oh, people say anything. Just gossip, it doesn't lead to anything . . .

MADELEINE: Until they find out and the trouble starts . . . We'll be the talk of the neighbourhood. And it won't stop at that!

AMÉDÉE: All right. I told you I'd get rid of him and I will. I
promise.

MADELEINE: When? When? When?

AMÉDÉE: Tomorrow . . . Let me have a little rest first.

MADELEINE: Tomorrow, tomorrow . . . I know your
promises, your 'tomorrows' . . . A whole life-time has
slipped away between your tomorrows . . . It's not tomorrow, it's this very day that you've got to make up your
mind. Understand?

AMÉDÉE: Very well. If you'd rather, I'll get rid of him for you
today.

MADELEINE: If only you meant it! [*A short silence.*] You do
intend to get rid of him for *both* of us, I suppose, and not just
for me? You'll do it a little for your own peace of mind,
too?

AMÉDÉE: Oh, if I was alone, you know, I'd get used to it
somehow.

MADELEINE: But where would you put him? Where would
you put him? This is such a tiny flat. We don't live in the
Louvre, full of long galleries you could shut a train in . . .
Even if we did, he'd fill them all.

AMÉDÉE: I only need a little space, a tiny little corner to live
in . . .

MADELEINE: You call that 'living' . . .

AMÉDÉE: Oh, leave me alone . . . It's just fate.

MADELEINE: You're quite hopeless . . . We haven't much
future left, you might at least try and make it a little more
pleasant . . . [*To herself*] What will people say! What *will*
people say!

AMÉDÉE: You don't give me a moment's peace . . . Do you
think I'm not suffering, too? I'm not the same as I used to
be, either. And you say I haven't changed!

MADELEINE: I've been telling you it's all your fault, and I'll
go on telling you until I can get it into your thick head.

AMÉDÉE [*weakly*]: No. It's not only *my* fault.

MADELEINE: It is, it is!

[AMÉDÉE, *beaten, shrugs his shoulders, says nothing, but*

59

*simply moves his lips to form the 'Tisn't' of an obstinate child;
it is quite inaudible. Silence.*]

You ought to have reported his death at the time. Or else
got rid of the body sooner, when it was easier. You can't
deny that you're lazy, idle, untidy . . .

AMÉDÉE: Dead tired, more than anything, dead tired.

MADELEINE [*continuing*]: You never know where you put
your own things. You waste three quarters of your time
looking for them, rummaging about in the drawers. And
then I find them for you under the bed, all over the place.
You're always taking on jobs you never finish. You make
plans, give them up and then let everything slide. If I
hadn't been here to keep us both alive . . . with the little I
earn . . . and now *that's* gone . . .

[*In his armchair or on the bed,* AMÉDÉE *suffers it all without a
word, crushed; his face, turned towards the audience, is expressive of immense fatigue.*]

MADELEINE [*taking it up again, after a pause*]: You've let
fifteen years go by . . . Fifteen years! . . . Now we'll never
make anyone believe that nothing's happening here, that
nothing's ever happened . . . And it's all because you've no
initiative . . . [*The dead man makes another sudden jerk forward.*
AMÉDÉE *rises painfully to his feet, like a robot, and goes to
measure the latest progress, makes a new chalk mark, returns to
his armchair, and falls heavily into it, while* MADELEINE, *with
hardly a pause, goes on with her tirade*] It might be better to tell
the police after all, if you won't do anything else . . .

AMÉDÉE: There'd be such a fuss . . .

MADELEINE: Anyway, if we could prove he'd been dead for
fifteen years . . . they can't prosecute when a man's been
dead for fifteen years . . .

AMÉDÉE: Thirteen . . .

MADELEINE: You see, even thirteen's enough, and in our
case it's fifteen . . . If you'd reported his death at the time,
we'd be all right now . . . We'd be feeling much safer . . .
Not so afraid of the neighbours. This place would be more
cheerful and we shouldn't be living like prisoners, like

criminals . . . [*She indicates the dead man.*] Because of him, everything goes wrong . . .

AMÉDÉE: I'll never succeed, Madeleine, in teaching you logic. If we'd gone to the authorities the day he died, we'd have been in prison long ago or probably been executed. The fifteen years would never have had time to elapse . . .

MADELEINE: Obviously I must be wrong. According to you I'm always wrong. But I still think . . . Yes, *I'm* always the stupid one, aren't I? That's what you're trying to say?

AMÉDÉE: I didn't mean you were stupid. It's just that you're not logical, which isn't the same thing at all.

MADELEINE: Oh! . . . you and your hair-splitting! . . .

AMÉDÉE: It's no good, we don't understand each other.

MADELEINE: I understand all right. And I've understood you too . . . for a very long time!

AMÉDÉE: I'm sure you have!

MADELEINE [*after a brief silence*]: Or perhaps you could still have gone to the police station the next day, after the murder, and told them you'd killed him in a fit of anger, out of jealousy. After all, it would have been perfectly true. You always said you thought he was my lover . . . And I never denied it . . .

AMÉDÉE: Oh? Is that why I killed him? I'd forgotten . . .

MADELEINE: Scatterbrain! As though anyone could forget a thing like that! [*Continuing*] . . . And as it was a crime of passion, you wouldn't have had any trouble; they'd have given you some little statement to sign and then let you go free. The statement would have been stuffed into a file, it would all be over and done with . . . the whole affair would have been forgotten ages ago . . .

AMÉDÉE: But as it is, we're still talking about it! . . . Poor young fellow . . . Ah yes! . . . I believe I remember, he had come to pay us a visit. Had I seen him before? Was it the first time he'd come to the flat?

MADELEINE [*continuing*]: I tell you we'd never have been in this state, if you hadn't been so careless and always let things slide.

AMÉDÉE: I've always loathed red tape and bureaucracy . . .

MADELEINE [*still sweeping on*]: Whenever I asked you, while there was still time, to go and register his death, you answered as you did just now: 'tomorrow', 'tomorrow', 'tomorrow', 'tomorrow' . . .

AMÉDÉE: I say, what if I went tomorrow?

MADELEINE [*forcefully*]: No! Today, today, today, today!

AMÉDÉE: Perhaps it's easier to go to the police station . . .

MADELEINE: Yes, easier than keeping your promise. Didn't you just say you were going to *get him out of here today*? Or do you want me to get a divorce?

AMÉDÉE: All right, all right . . . *today* . . .

MADELEINE: Anyway, I can't see *you* going to the police station. Besides, it wouldn't do any good now. Fifteen years after the murder, they'd never believe you did it in anger. If you wait fifteen years, that proves it was premeditated . . .

AMÉDÉE: Look here, Madeleine . . .

MADELEINE: If you're going to tell me again I'm not logical!

AMÉDÉE: I'm not.

MADELEINE: Well, what is it, then?

AMÉDÉE: I'm wondering what we could say to the police . . . As he's grown so old – he does look very old, doesn't he? – perhaps I could say it was my father and I killed him yesterday . . .

MADELEINE: Oh, I don't think that'd be a very bright idea . . .

AMÉDÉE: No, perhaps not. You're right . . .

MADELEINE: Officially, there's nothing we can do now. But we can still get round the law. You've got to act on your own . . . and as quickly as possible . . .

AMÉDÉE [*gets up slowly and walks round the walls of the room, avoiding the body*]: In point of fact, Madeleine, I'm just wondering if I really . . .

MADELEINE: What's the matter now? You're hesitating, aren't you? You don't want to do anything!

AMÉDÉE: Yes I do. I was going to say something else.

MADELEINE: What then? What's puzzling you?

AMÉDÉE: Did I really kill him?

MADELEINE: You don't think it was a poor weak woman . . . like me?

AMÉDÉE: No, no. Of course not.

MADELEINE: Well?

AMÉDÉE: Was it really this young Romeo that we . . . that I killed? It seems to me, – oh, what a memory I've got! . . . it seems to me that the young man had already left . . . when the crime was committed . . .

MADELEINE: You admitted yourself you'd killed him. You said you remembered. You did, didn't you?

AMÉDÉE: Perhaps I was wrong. I may have been mistaken . . . I get everything so mixed up, dreams and real life, memories and imagination . . . Now I don't know where I am.

MADELEINE: If it's not the young man, who else could it possibly have been?

AMÉDÉE: Perhaps it was the baby.

MADELEINE: The baby?

AMÉDÉE: A neighbour once asked us to look after a baby. Do you remember? It was years ago. She never came to take it away . . .

MADELEINE: What nonsense! . . . Why should the baby have died? And why, if it did die, did we keep it here and let it grow up? How careless can you get? And where would you have killed it? . . . Murderer! Baby-killer!

AMÉDÉE: It's possible. I don't know. Perhaps it was crying too loud? Crying babies get on my nerves . . . It must have stopped me working, writing my play. I suppose it must have infuriated me so much, that baby squalling away hour after hour, that I . . . in a fit of justifiable rage . . . a clumsy blow . . . a bit brutal . . . killing babies is as easy as killing flies, you know!

MADELEINE: Whether this old man's really the baby or the young lover doesn't alter the situation. And you've got to get us out of it.

AMÉDÉE: Of course, of course! . . . [*A second later, his face lit up by a glimmering of hope.*] But why shouldn't he have died a natural death anyway? Why do you insist I killed him? A baby's very delicate. It holds to life by a thread.

MADELEINE: It wasn't the baby. My memory's more reliable than yours. It was the young man.

AMÉDÉE: A young lover . . . a lover . . . who comes in . . . drinks a bit too much . . . sees a pretty woman . . . quite voluptuous . . . *that* sends up the blood-pressure . . . a stroke perhaps and . . . good Lord . . .

MADELEINE: So it's all my fault? That's what you mean, isn't it . . . I thought we'd agreed it was nothing to do with me! . . .

AMÉDÉE: I'm sorry.

MADELEINE: To start with, it takes more than *that* to kill a young man of twenty. *He* doesn't suffer from hardening of the arteries, like one old crock I know . . .

[*When she says 'old crock'* MADELEINE *stresses these two words and glances significantly at Amédée; the latter pretends not to understand.*]

AMÉDÉE: Now I come to think of it, I'm not sure it wasn't someone else . . .

MADELEINE: Who then? What are you getting at now?

AMÉDÉE: Listen . . . You know I was in the country one day fishing . . . a woman fell in the water and shouted for help. As I can't swim – and anyway the fish were biting – I stayed where I was and left her to drown. . . . In that case I'd merely be charged with not helping someone whose life was in danger. . . . That's not so serious.

MADELEINE: And how would you explain the presence of this corpse in our flat?

AMÉDÉE: Oh! . . . I don't know about that. It might have been brought here for artificial respiration . . . Or it could have come by itself . . .

MADELEINE: Idiot! You've forgotten it's not the body of a woman, it's a man's!

AMÉDÉE: That's true. I hadn't thought of that.

MADELEINE: In any case, we'd still be guilty of harbouring a corpse.

AMÉDÉE: Yes, you're right there . . . quite right . . . [*A pause. He goes on thinking, walking round the walls of the room; he accidentally bumps into a mushroom, or crushes it; he gives a start.*] I beg your pardon!

[MADELEINE *has seen it coming, too late.*]

MADELEINE [*losing her temper*]: Mind my mushrooms! . . . I suppose you're going to squash all my mushrooms, now!

AMÉDÉE: I didn't do it on purpose!

MADELEINE: Poor little mushrooms! You've broken all the crockery already! Now there's not a plate left for you to practise your clumsiness on . . .

AMÉDÉE: You know, you can't practise clumsiness . . .

MADELEINE: . . . you're having a go at my mushrooms!

AMÉDÉE: There are plenty of them, anyway. Look how they're springing up, and getting fatter all the time . . .

MADELEINE: You said there'd always be plenty of my plates too . . . and now there's not one left . . .

AMÉDÉE: Plates don't grow . . .

MADELEINE: No, but they cost money.

AMÉDÉE: Whereas mushrooms, they just germinate and shoot up . . . At least, as long as *he's* here . . . [*He points to the body.*]

MADELEINE: Another reason for leaving him here, I suppose . . .

AMÉDÉE: No, no! Of course not . . .

[*The dead man's feet slide forward suddenly in several successive jerks; they advance a long way towards the right-hand door, very noisily as usual.*]

MADELEINE [*letting out a distracted cry*]: Ah! Amédée! You see! You see! What on earth are you waiting for!

[AMÉDÉE *tries to mark the fresh progress with the chalk, but gives it up when the body jerks forward again; he throws the chalk aside and shrugs his shoulders.*]

What are you waiting for? What are you hoping for? Make up your mind, can't you?

AMÉDÉE: Yes, I see I must. I see I must . . . It's not going to be easy.

MADELEINE: Please, please darling, do something . . .

AMÉDÉE: What did you say?

MADELEINE [*annoyed again*]: I simply said 'Do something', because something has got to be done, that's all. . . . And I said it because it's up to you.

AMÉDÉE: I can't do it straightaway. I must wait till it's dark. Tonight's the time. That's a promise.

MADELEINE: What a relief it will be.

AMÉDÉE: You'll be happy at last.

MADELEINE: Happy . . . Happy . . . As if we could make up for all that lost time! All those wasted years, they're a dead weight . . . always with us . . .

AMÉDÉE: It'll be some consolation, anyway.

MADELEINE: I shan't be quite so miserable in my old age, that's all . . .

AMÉDÉE: If you like, perhaps we *could* try and remove him at once . . .

MADELEINE: It's too risky, for both of us. No one must see you. Let's wait till it's dark. What's it matter . . . It should have been done long ago . . . we'll have to wait a little longer, until this evening . . . we've waited for fifteen years . . . what are a few hours more? Oh dear, I'm so used to waiting, waiting, waiting, long uncomfortable years of waiting, that's what my life has been . . .

AMÉDÉE [*timidly*]: So has mine.

MADELEINE: . . . that's what my life has been . . . you could write a book about it! Why have you never thought of writing a novel about my life? Surely, I've earned it. You never think of me!

AMÉDÉE [*timidly*]: I'll try, if you like . . . after we've . . .

[*The dead man advances slightly; from now on the body will advance, slowly but steadily, towards the right-hand door, but without jerking.*]

MADELEINE: If he's still got geometrical progression, will the flat hold him until tonight?

AMÉDÉE: Well, I hope so . . . [*He makes a rough mental calculation of the distance separating the feet from the right-hand wall.*]

MADELEINE: You might work it out. Then we'd be sure . . .

AMÉDÉE [*with a tired gesture*]: I was never very good at maths. We'll soon see . . .

MADELEINE: You're never sure of anything, are you?

AMÉDÉE: Let's sit down. Keep our strength up. And wait. We can't help it. Can't do anything else. Sit down, Madeleine . . . We've got to make the best of it.

[MADELEINE *and* AMÉDÉE *sit down, he collapsing into his armchair, she nervously on the edge of a chair. Silence. Then, picking up her needles, she starts knitting, impatiently; from time to time she glances at Amédée, then stares at the clock at the back of the stage. The audience should still be able to see its hands, moving slowly at the same speed as the dead man's feet. Meanwhile the room where the two characters are sitting will grow dim as the light through the rear window changes from daylight to a sunset glow, later becoming almost dark in the twilight; right at the end of the act there will be moonlight, coming from a huge, round moon that can be seen through the window.*]

MADELEINE [*another glance at Amédée, then at the clock. Silence. She is knitting. She looks again at Amédée, who is crumpled in his armchair, facing the audience, with his eyes half-closed; she opens her mouth to say something, then shuts it again. The clock strikes the hour; once more, she looks at Amédée and then*]: Amédée!

AMÉDÉE [*his eyes still closed*]: What? ! . . . Let me get my strength back . . .

MADELEINE: You ought to get on with some work . . . it'll help you to pass the time until the evening . . . Write your play . . . It'd be a shame to miss an opportunity like this . . .

AMÉDÉE [*as before*]: . . . I'm . . . so . . . tired . . .

MADELEINE: Make an effort, Amédée! You know it's for your own good . . .

AMÉDÉE [*as before*]: No energy, not up to the mark . . . I can't . . . no . . . really . . . not just now . . .

MADELEINE: But you've nothing else to do until tonight . . .

[*Silence;* AMÉDÉE *tries to stand up, half rises and falls back*

*into the armchair again. Heavy silence; the body is still imper-
ceptibly lengthening, the hands of the clock are gradually
advancing.*]

AMÉDÉE [*as before*]: It's such a long time until tonight. . . .
I'm scared stiff already . . .

MADELEINE [*less harshly*]: Courage, Amédée. Keep calm and
you'll forget you're frightened. Control yourself.

AMÉDÉE [*as before*]: I'll try and control myself.

MADELEINE: It's the only way.

[*Silence.*]

AMÉDÉE [*as before*]: It's going to be a tremendous effort to
carry him . . . it'll take it out of me . . .

MADELEINE: Try not to think about it . . . think about something else . . . forget about it till later . . . don't waste your
energy. Do a little writing . . .

AMÉDÉE [*as before*]: Forget . . . when that's all we're waiting
for, just waiting for time to pass . . . I've got palpitations
already . . .

MADELEINE: It'll be a nasty moment . . . but I'll be there,
I'll help you.

AMÉDÉE [*as before*]: The worst part, the worst part of all, I'll
have to do myself . . .

MADELEINE: Well, it's your turn now.

AMÉDÉE: . . . and the most dangerous part . . .

MADELEINE: It's just as dangerous for both of us . . .

AMÉDÉE [*as before*]: . . . And the physical effort . . .

MADELEINE: You're a man.

AMÉDÉE [*as before*]: I never went in for sport. I never did any
manual labour. I'm no good, even at odd jobs. I've a
sedentary occupation, I'm an intellectual . . .

MADELEINE: You never had a proper education or you'd
have kept fit . . .

AMÉDÉE [*as before*]: I realize that now . . . too late, too late
. . . But whoever would have dreamt . . . that I should
have to . . .

MADELEINE: You have to be ready for everything in life, for
any eventuality . . .

AMÉDÉE [*as before*]: That's true. My parents didn't look ahead . . . No use blaming them now . . .

MADELEINE [*more nervously*]: And yet at times, usually the wrong times, you do have bursts of energy . . . You managed to kill him all right . . . Pity your strength didn't fail you then, you might have had a bit more today!

AMÉDÉE [*as before*]: Listen, there's no real proof I did kill him. I'm not at all sure I did.

MADELEINE: Off you go again!

AMÉDÉE [*as before*]: But I told you before!

MADELEINE: Are you crazy or just being awkward?

AMÉDÉE [*as before*]: I'm willing to admit it, as I can't see any other reasonable explanation . . . I admit it *looks* as if I was the one who killed him . . .

MADELEINE: Well, that's something! . . .

AMÉDÉE [*as before*]: But it's so easy to find the energy, the sudden strength you need, to kill someone in a fit of spite or anger . . . It just *happens* . . . Anybody could do it . . . It's the prolonged physical effort that frightens me . . . Will it be too much for me? . . . The physical effort, the mere thought of it, the premeditated effort, the waiting, that's what's killing me. [*Sighing*] I will do it, because I must . . . because I must . . .

MADELEINE: It's all quite simple, then. Try and stop worrying. That'll help. Pretend nothing's the matter. This is a day like any other . . . just as dreary but no drearier . . . Write your play. That'll put the neighbours off the scent as well. We mustn't give them the slightest suspicion . . .

AMÉDÉE [*as before*]: No need to worry about the neighbours. They're not thinking abut us. Listen . . . not a sound . . .

MADELEINE: They're there all right. No fear of that. In their flats, with their ears glued to the walls or the floorboards, or at their windows, peering out, perhaps, behind the curtains . . . or downstairs, in silent groups, standing round the concierge . . .

AMÉDÉE [*as before*]: You're exaggerating . . .

MADELEINE: I know them better than you do. It's when

they're quiet I fear them most. People are so cruel, with their callous curiosity ... They're always spying on us, they do nothing else all day. Can't you *feel* them there? Can't you sense how heavy the silence is? As soon as they've anything to go on, this uneasy silence you've such faith in will shatter like a vase into a thousand fragments ... I'd much rather they were talking, making sure their nasty remarks are loud enough for us to hear ... or even slipping their dirty little notes under the door ... or trying to make holes in the wall to put bits of wire through ... you know, as they did the other day ... I prefer that any time. You know where you stand ... But this sinister silence of theirs, I can't get used to it ... We must be on our guard ...

AMÉDÉE [*as before*]: This evening ... tonight ... at midnight, the witching hour, not before ... like a thief ... If only we could get started ... get it over ... Oh! If only the time would pass more quickly! [*Silence*] We've just got to make the best of it.

[*Silence.*]

MADELEINE [*suddenly*]: Oh, for goodness' sake do a little work! How many times have I got to tell you? Don't you realize we must keep them guessing? ... As though there was nothing unusual. ...

AMÉDÉE [*still in the same position, laboriously*]: Just a day like any other, any other day ...

MADELEINE: Oh, write something, do! ... pull yourself together! [*Indicating the body*] Surely *he* ought to inspire you, concentrate ... I haven't much heart for work either ... but I'm going on with my knitting, as usual ...

AMÉDÉE [*as before*]: I'll try. I must get down to it, must get down to it ... [*Silence.*] Why, I believe ... I believe ... the images are rising ... painfully lifting their heads ... the words are taking flight ... everything's on the move ... coming slowly nearer ... how tired I am! ... funny sort of job ... [*With great scorn*] A writer ... [*Short pause*] I'd rather sleep, until midnight. But I couldn't anyway ... no more sleep for me ... I – must – write! [*Short pause. Still in*

the same position.] The horizon's a ring of dark mountains ...
Thick clouds are sweeping over the ground ... smoke and
mist ... That's it ... Come closer, come on, closer ...
[*Still in the same position, his eyes half shut, he appears to be pulling something very heavy towards him with an invisible rope; he
opens his eyes for a few seconds and his face should express
immense weariness; he does not change his attitude, he is still
crumpled in his armchair facing the audience, and when he pulls the
invisible rope, he does so very slowly. He is like a man so exhausted
and overtaxed that any effort, especially this, is extremely painful.
At the same time he is rocking his head and shoulders rhythmically
from the left to right, from right to left, in the chair; he should look
as though, at any moment, his head, which is swaying backwards and forwards, might snap from his neck and go rolling into
the laps of the people in the first row of the stalls.*] Come out ... of
the well ... come out ... come up ... that's right ... now
I can just see their faces ... im-a-ges ... im-a-ges ...
what, what, what are they like ... there they are ...
[*While* MADELEINE *goes on knitting in her corner, two
figures, two actors, come in or appear from the back of the stage,
and move round on the same spot during the following scene.
They are made up realistically to look like Amédée and
Madeleine, whose voices they carefully imitate; in the end their
voices will be very shrill, especially that of* MADELEINE II,
*plaintive, inhuman, unreal, like the cry of animals in pain.
When their doubles appear,* MADELEINE *will go on knitting
where she sits and* AMÉDÉE *will stay in his armchair or on his
bed for a while, still pulling at his imaginary rope and rhythmically swaying his head and shoulders, before he finally and
gradually becomes motionless. When he is quite still, his eyes
half closed, with a fixed expression of gloom and weariness on
his face, he could for example, stay for a moment with his mouth
half open. He should – except for his interruptions and at the
end of the scene – appear as detached as Madeleine from what is
happening on the stage. It should be pointed out that, so far as
possible, Madeleine II and Amédée II should not be made
to look like ectoplasm; to avoid this, they should not appear in a*

ghostly glow, but in the normal lighting for the scene. Madeleine II and Amédée II should play their parts quite naturally in this unnatural and unreal situation – just as naturally as Amédée and Madeleine play theirs.

In case of production difficulties, and especially if it is impossible to find two actors exactly resembling those who are playing Amédée and Madeleine, this scene can be played as follows: attention is concentrated on Amédée, so that nothing is seen but his still face; MADELEINE *has disappeared; music; the light intensifies, suggesting a festive occasion.* AMÉDÉE *is a young bridegroom: he takes from a drawer white gloves, hat, tie, flowers etc. and dresses.* MADELEINE *appears on the balcony, facing the audience, as a bride, veiled perhaps. Music.* AMÉDÉE, *looking very young, moves towards her. If this second possibility is adopted, there is obviously no need for extra actors: in such case the dialogue that appears in brackets may also be suppressed.*]

AMÉDÉE II: Madeleine, Madeleine!

MADELEINE II: Don't come near me. Don't touch me. You sting, sting, sting. You hu-urt me! What do you wa-ant! Where are you going, going, going?

AMÉDÉE II: Madeleine . . .

MADELEINE II [*half wailing, half shouting*]: Aaaah! Aaah! Aaah!

AMÉDÉE II: Madeleine, wake up, let's pull the curtains, the spring is dawning . . . Wake up . . . the room is flooded with sunshine . . . a glorious light . . . a gentle warmth! . . .

MADELEINE II: . . . night and rain and mud! . . . oh, the cold! . . . I'm shivering . . . dark . . . dark . . . dark! . . . you're blind, you're gilding reality! Don't you see that you're *making* it beautiful?

AMÉDÉE II: It's reality that makes us beautiful.

MADELEINE II: Good God, he's mad! he's mad! My husband's mad! !

AMÉDÉE II: Look . . . look . . . gaze into your memories, into the present and the future . . . look around you!

MADELEINE II: I can see nothing . . . It's dark . . . there's nothing . . . I can see nothing! . . . You're blind!

AMÉDÉE II: No, I can see, I can see . . .

MADELEINE II: No . . . no . . . no . . .

AMÉDÉE II: . . . The green valley where the lilies bloom . . .

MADELEINE II: Mushrooms! . . . mushrooms! . . . mushrooms! . . . mushrooms! . . .

AMÉDÉE II: Yes, in the green valley . . . they're dancing in a ring, hand in hand . . .

MADELEINE II: A damp dark valley, a marsh that sucks you down until you drown . . . help! help! I'm suffocating, help! . . .

AMÉDÉE II: I'm bursting with song . . . la, li, la, li, la, la, la!

MADELEINE II: Stop singing in that cracked voice . . . It's ear-splitting!

AMÉDÉE II: La, li, la, li, la, la, la! . . .

MADELEINE II: Stop shrieking . . . stop shri-e-king! . . . your voice is so piercing! You're deafening me! Hu-urting me! Don't rend my darkness! S-a-dist! S-a-dist!

AMÉDÉE II: Madeleine, darling . . .

MADELEINE II: Amédée, wretch!

AMÉDÉE II: Madeleine, you used to sing once!

MADELEINE II: Because I was bored, popular songs, only because I was bored!

AMÉDÉE II: Let's dance! . . . Round and round . . . In a blaze of joy . . . The light's gone mad . . . Love's gone mad . . . Mad with happiness . . . Blaze up, joy, blaze up!

MADELEINE II: Don't shoot! . . . Don't shoot! . . . Bayonets and machine-guns . . . Don't shoot, I'm afraid! . . .

AMÉDÉE II: Everyone's embracing.

MADELEINE II: Don't kill me . . . Have mercy, I implore you . . . don't kill him, don't kill them . . . , have mercy on the children! . . .

AMÉDÉE II: Mad with happiness . . .

MADELEINE II: Madness! Madness! Madness!

AMÉDÉE II: We're floating across a limpid lake. Our boat a

bed of flowers ... rocked along ... slipping over the waters ...

MADELEINE II [*a cry of terror*]: I'm sl-i-pping! ... A boat? What boat? What boat are you talking about? Which boat can you mean? Where can you see any b-o-a-ts! ... Hee! Hee! Hee! Hee! Boats bogged in the mud, in the desert sand, can it be true?

AMÉDÉE II: White churches! ... Bells pealing! ... Churches that are doves! ...

MADELEINE II: Bells! What bells? ... I can hear nothing! You're deaf, there's nothing, you're deaf ...

AMÉDÉE II: Children's voices! ... voices of fountains ... voices of spring!

MADELEINE II: No, no, they're oaths and toads!

AMÉDÉE II: The voice of the snows on the mountain ...

MADELEINE II: Forests of slime, nights in the hulks! ... forests of hell ... Oh! Leave me alone! Let me go! ... Aaah! ... Nightmare! ...

AMÉDÉE II: The horizon is breathing. Glorious light ...

MADELEINE II: Where? Where? Beware! Beware! Of the clouds and the wolves! Beware!

AMÉDÉE II: The morning never grows old ... Sparkling radiance ... The night is over ... over ...

MADELEINE II: I'm sinking into the darkness! Heavy shades of night! ... Cut them with a knife ... I won't, I won't ... I'm frightened! Aaah! ...

AMÉDÉE II: Madeleine ...

MADELEINE II: Who makes these brittle leaves grow on the trees, these stinging branches and clinging creepers?! It's you! You horrible b-e-ast!

AMÉDÉE II: Madeleine, my own little girl ...

MADELEINE II: They're lashing my cheeks, my shoulders! It's you, you devil, it's you who struck me in the face! You br-u-te!!

AMÉDÉE II: There's nothing in the way. There aren't any trees. Look carefully ... Look ... Stones as soft as moss ...

MADELEINE II: They blister my feet . . . Thorns of fire! Flames like needles, flames of ice . . . they're digging redhot pins into my flesh. Aaah!

AMÉDÉE II: If only you wished . . . Nature would be so bountiful. . . . wings on our feet, our limbs like wings . . . our shoulders wings . . . gravity abolished . . . no more weariness . . .

MADELEINE II: Night . . . always night . . . alone in the world! . . .

AMÉDÉE II: We are at the gates of the world!

MADELEINE II [*parrot-like*]: Fancy that! Fancy that! There's no such thing! Never satisfied! Never satisfied!

AMÉDÉE II: An insubstantial universe . . . Freedom . . . Ethereal power . . . Balance . . . airy abundance . . . world without weight . . .

MADELEINE II: Fancy that! Fancy that!

AMÉDÉE II: You could lift the world with one hand . . .

MADELEINE II: Never satisfied! Never satisfied!

[AMÉDÉE [*in his armchair*]: Time is heavy. The world dense. The years brief. The seconds slow.]

MADELEINE II: Stone is just space. Walls are a void. There is nothing . . . nothing . . .

[AMÉDÉE [*in his armchair*]: It's heavy. Yet it's so badly stuck together. . . . Nothing but holes . . . the walls are tottering, the leaden mass subsides!]

MADELEINE II: It's going to collapse about our ears! . . . It's fallen on my head! . . . Oh! . . . those filthy mushrooms, they stink, they're rotting everything away!

AMÉDÉE II: Every voice echoes ours. Everything corresponds. We take each other by the hand. There is space, but no distance!

MADELEINE II: I am a widow, I am an orphan, I am poor, sick, old, the oldest orphan in the world!

AMÉDÉE II: Every dawn is a victory! . . . Every sun is rising . . .

MADELEINE II: Never satisfied, wretched man, fancy that, never satisfied . . .

[AMÉDÉE [*in his armchair*]: It's soon going to break right up, into pieces . . .]

AMÉDÉE II: Try to remember, remember . . .

MADELEINE II: Don't say that! Don't say that! Never satisfied!

AMÉDÉE II: The sparrows grew strong again in our hands, the flowers never faded.

MADELEINE II: What imagination! What imagination! When? Tell me when? You get on my nerves . . . on my nerves . . . It can't be! . . . not true, never true. . . . All wrong, all wrong!

AMÉDÉE II: You are so beautiful, a queen of beauty!

MADELEINE II: A queen of beauty! Fancy that! . . . Who have you mistaken me for, you wretch? He's making fun of me, making fun of my nose! Haven't you noticed my nose?

AMÉDÉE II: You've lost your memory, find it again, find your memory . . .

MADELEINE II: Don't say that. You get on my nerves. Never satisfied. Wretched man. Beautiful, a queen of beauty, fancy that!

AMÉDÉE II: What is far can be near. What is withered can grow green again. What is separated can be reunited. What *is* no longer will *be* again.

MADELEINE II: It's not true! It's not true! Stop saying that. You're breaking my heart!

AMÉDÉE II: We love each other. We are happy. In a house of glass, a house of light . . .

MADELEINE II: He means a house of brass, brass . . .

AMÉDÉE II: House of glass, of light . . .

MADELEINE II: House of brass, house of night!

AMÉDÉE II: Of glass, of light, of glass, of light . . .

MADELEINE II: Of brass, of brass, of night, of brass, of night . . .

AMÉDÉE II: Of glass, glass, glass . . .

MADELEINE II: Brass, night, brass, night, brass, night . . . brass, brass, brass, brass, brass . . .

AMÉDÉE II: [*as though beaten*]: Glass, light, glass, light ...
brass, light, brass, night, night, brass ...

AMÉDÉE II *and* MADELEINE II: Brass, night, brass, night,
brass, night, brass, night ...

AMÉDÉE II: The brass and the night, alas ...

MADELEINE II: Aaah! Aaah! [*Sobbing*] ... Fire and ice ...
Fire ... deep down within me. It's all around me. All
about me ... inside and out! ... I'm burning! Help me
... Alidulée! ...

AMÉDÉE II *and* MADELEINE II: Alidulée ... Alidulée ...
Alidulée! ... Help, Alidulée! ... Alidulée ... Alidulée
... Alidulée Love ... Alidulée Love ... Dear Alidulée
... Help, Alidulée ... Alidulée! ...

[MADELEINE II *rushes out screaming;* AMÉDÉE II *runs
after her shouting:* 'Wait for me! Wait for me!' *The
doubles have disappeared.* MADELEINE *rises briskly and
addresses* AMÉDÉE *in his armchair.*

If there are no doubles: MADELEINE *rushes out screaming.*
AMÉDÉE *remains alone. He looks sad. He returns slowly to his
table, and takes off his hat and gloves.* AMÉDÉE *has grown old
again. The same atmosphere as at the beginning of the second
act.* MADELEINE *re-enters from the back of the stage, goes and
takes up her knitting, and, in a scolding mood, speaks from where
she is sitting.*]

AMÉDÉE [*in the same position as before*]: Is it time?

MADELEINE [*in the same position as before*]: No. It's not time
yet.

AMÉDÉE [*as before*]: Is it getting near?

MADELEINE [*as before*]: Not really. Patience, a little patience.

AMÉDÉE [*to Madeleine*]: Poor Madeleine! What a terrible
time you've had. [*Looking as though he wishes to approach her*]
Do you know, Madeleine, if we loved each other, if we
really loved each other, none of this would be important.
[*Clasping his hands*] Why don't we try to love each other,
please, Madeleine? Love puts everything right, you know,
it changes life. Do you believe me, can you understand?

MADELEINE: Oh! Leave me alone!

AMÉDÉE [*stammering*]: I know it does! . . . Love makes up for everything.

MADELEINE: Don't talk rubbish! I can't see love getting rid of this dead body. Nor hate either, for that matter. It's got nothing to do with feelings.

AMÉDÉE: I'll get rid of it for you . . .

MADELEINE: It just doesn't make sense! Where does love come into it? Lot of nonsense! Love can't help people get rid of their troubles! You know nothing about real people! When are you going to write an ordinary sort of play?

AMÉDÉE [*as before*]: It's just the way it turns out. After all, I wanted to write a sociological play.

MADELEINE: When you *do* have inspiration, it's always morbid. There's nothing true about it . . . Real life's not like that.

AMÉDÉE [*as before*]: There must be something in the atmosphere . . .

MADELEINE: It doesn't sound like you at all, not like your real self! [*Pointing to the body*] It's his fault. It all comes from him. *He* must have given you the idea. It's *his* world, not *ours*.

AMÉDÉE [*as before*]: Yes, perhaps you're . . .

MADELEINE: He interferes in everything, don't you realize?

AMÉDÉE [*as before*]: Perhaps.

MADELEINE: There's no doubt about it! [*She slips on the floor.*] It's all slippery . . . The mushrooms are sprouting all over the floor . . . And love won't sweep it clean either . . . [*Glances towards the open door of the room*] Now we can't even shut the door. He's invaded the whole place! No need to leave his eyes open anyway . . . You still haven't closed them . . .

AMÉDÉE [*as before*]: I'll go and do it . . . [*He sits quite still.*]

[*In any case he hardly has the time, for suddenly strange music is heard coming from the dead man's room and gradually growing louder; the stage is dark by now and it is eight by the clock. AMÉDÉE and MADELEINE listen in silence and without a movement in the deepening gloom, which is gradually replaced by a green glow issuing from the bedroom. Other sounds made by the neighbours will be heard while the music is playing: a distant 'Supper's ready!' and the noise of a bell ringing; muffled footsteps on the stairs; the chinking of plates and glasses – it is supper-time; then these sounds slowly fade until only the music is heard. At one moment, just after the music has started,* AMÉDÉE *gets up and furtively changes the position of a piece of furniture to make room for the body, which is still growing; then he goes and sits down next to Madeleine amongst the lumber and they both go on listening there, in silence, to the dead man's strange music, both hidden from the audience. In order to reach this position – and to leave it again at the end of the scene – first* AMÉDÉE, *then* AMÉDÉE *and* MADELEINE, *find it difficult to move, as the dead man has been growing and is about to fill up all the available space; later on* AMÉDÉE *and* MADELEINE *have to pass between the dead man's feet and the furniture or between his feet and the right-hand door, and this move almost calls for acrobatics. The music should be heard for a long time; stress must be laid on the green light, the jumbled furniture, and the stage empty of characters, for Amédée and Madeleine are hidden by all the lumber for a considerable period; so, in this scene, what is important is the music, the advancing feet of the dead man, and the green light.*]

MADELEINE [*at the very first faint note of music*]: What's that? Do you hear? I suppose it's that play of yours again!

AMÉDÉE: No. Keet quiet. It's him, he's singing.

MADELEINE [*in a lower voice*]: But his mouth is shut . . .

AMÉDÉE [*also in a low voice*]: I expect the sounds are coming out of his ears . . . they're the best musical instrument of all . . .

[*The striking of the clock chimes in with the music. Pause. Then the outside noises start up.*]

MADELEINE [*as before*]: It's coming from all directions at once . . .

AMÉDÉE [*as before*]: Each wave of sound gives birth to another . . . it shows how strong he is . . .

[AMÉDÉE *and* MADELEINE *are silent. For a time there is*

79

nothing but the music, then the stage, which is almost completely dark, is suddenly lit by a not unpleasant green light that comes from the dead man's room and first illuminates only one side of the stage.]

MADELEINE: . . . The light's coming from his room. [*Softly*] That's where it's coming from all right.

AMÉDÉE [*softly*]: It's his eyes shining . . . like two beacons . . . all the better, we don't have to put the lamp on . . . his light is softer.

MADELEINE: Close the shutters.

[AMÉDÉE *goes and closes the shutters very quietly.*]

AMÉDÉE: The neighbours will have finished their supper soon. They'll be going to bed.

MADELEINE [*still in a low voice, while* AMÉDÉE *comes back to her side in silence*]: Well, I must admit he's not without talent. [*A long pause; a long spell of music; the hands of the clock stand out against the dark background; moonlight steals through the slats in the shutters. Then suddenly, without a word,* AMÉDÉE *and* MADELEINE *rise simultaneously to their feet, a good few moments after the last note of music has sounded.*]

MADELEINE: We ought to move the wardrobe.

AMÉDÉE: Oh dear! He'll soon reach the door.

MADELEINE: You don't want him to go through it, do you? [*Distracted, but silent,* AMÉDÉE *and* MADELEINE *carry out a series of wordless movements, while the hands of the clock go round faster. They shift the wardrobe in silence; their movements are wild and unsystematic; they change the position of other pieces of furniture, clambering with difficulty from one side of the dead man's legs to the other. In their frenzy it is, however,* AMÉDÉE *who is the calmer or more deliberate of the two. Then* MADELEINE *polishes the dead man's shoes with a duster.* AMÉDÉE *brushes the trousers down with his hand and then adjusts the position of the feet on a stool.* MADELEINE *puts back into the wardrobe she has just moved the duster she had taken out to polish the shoes. At a certain moment, while there is no change in* MADELEINE'S *agitation,* AMÉDÉE *stands still, his back to the audience, his hands clasped behind his back and gazes at the*

*dead man's feet; then his glance slowly wanders the whole length
of the body to rest for a moment on the open door. He turns round
again, sighing and shaking his head. For a brief space*
MADELEINE *looks at* AMÉDÉE *without speaking; she seems
quite cast down and makes a gesture in his direction as if to say:
'You see what we've come to now'. Then a fresh burst of activity,
as both characters move haphazardly about the stage, this time
empty-handed. This silent, aimless scurrying is sharply inter-
rupted by the violent sound of a gong: the dead man's feet have
reached the door. The actors' movements become slower at once,
visibly so, and are once more heavy and dragging.*]

MADELEINE [*at the sound of the gong*]: He's reached the door.
It's time. Are you still as tired?

AMÉDÉE: Have I time to collect my strength? [*He is standing
motionless opposite the left-hand door.*]

MADELEINE: It would have been more sensible of you to
rest, instead of dashing about like that.

AMÉDÉE: It's a long time since rest did me any good. Or
even sleep. When I get up I'm more exhausted than when
I went to bed . . . To think I once had so much vim and
vigour!

MADELEINE: You're dreaming again. Vim and vigour! You!

AMÉDÉE [*in the same attitude*]: Oh yes, me . . . It's not fair to
say that . . . I used to bend iron bars with my bare hands
and lift carts with my shoulders. Nowadays, even a feather
weighs a ton . . .

MADELEINE: To hear you talk, you'd think I'd married Mr
Universe . . .

[*The clock shows a quarter to midnight.*]

AMÉDÉE: Has the time really come . . .?

MADELEINE: Yes, it has . . .

AMÉDÉE [*walks heavily to the window, while* MADELEINE
watches him]: So the moment's come at last!

MADELEINE: You've still got a minute or two.

AMÉDÉE [*looking through the slats in the shutters*]: Now there's
not a soul in sight.

MADELEINE: Don't look. Someone might see you.

AMÉDÉE [*looking at the dead man's feet*]: His feet are right against the door.

MADELEINE: So long as they don't go through. It leads on to the landing. We'd be done for . . . Mind that armchair . . .

   [AMÉDÉE *and* MADELEINE *move the armchair; they push the feet sideways a little, to the right or the left.*]

A little more . . . Push.

   [AMÉDÉE *does so.*]

That'll do . . . There! . . .

AMÉDÉE: Do you think it'll really do any good to get rid of him? What if another guest turns up, and the whole thing starts all over again? . . .

MADELEINE: He'd be smaller, anyway. He wouldn't take up all the room, not at first. We'd have time to breathe before he grew.

AMÉDÉE: That's true . . . A few years of comparative peace; that'd be something . . . [*Gazing towards the room*] He looks older than he did just now . . .

   [*He is still standing face to the room, while* MADELEINE *has collapsed into the armchair. Pause.*]

He's still good-looking, though. [*Pause.*] It's funny how, in spite of everything, I'd got used to him.

MADELEINE: So had I . . . But that's no reason for keeping him here. Look at the clock. The moment's arrived. Now's the time.

AMÉDÉE [*from the same spot*]: I know. Once a thing's settled, it's settled. I'm not going back on my word. But I must say that the thought of saying good-bye to him . . . Yes . . . I'll be quite sorry to see him go . . . [*He walks a few steps and gently pushes a pedestal table out of the way, to make room for the feet.*] This door's a good bit stronger than the other one, anyhow. [*Walking round the stage, hands clasped behind hunched shoulders.*] If he'd behaved properly, we might have kept him. After all, he's grown up and grown old with us in this house. That counts for something! You can't help it, you get attached to things, human beings are like that . . . Yes, you can get attached to almost anything . . . to a dog, a cat, a box, a child ... especially to him, there was every reason ... What memories he brings back ... Our home will seem quite empty when he's gone ... He's been the silent witness of our whole past, which hasn't always been so pleasant, I admit ... you might almost say: *because* of him ... but then life is never very cheerful ... if it's not one thing, it's another. What I mean is ... Perhaps we didn't know how to cope with the situation, we ought to have taken it more philosophically. All this might have turned out differently, not much better, of course, but we ought to have tried to accept things ... We never tried everything, never did all we could to make him feel at home ... We've all behaved badly at some time or other, so we ought to be more tolerant ... Otherwise, otherwise, life is impossible. ... We can't be expected to understand everything ... so we ought to be more broad-minded ...

MADELEINE: You're not hesitating again at the last moment. You're not going to back out.

AMÉDÉE [*with a sigh*]: There's no other way.

[*Another gong-like blow against the door; the clock strikes midnight.*]

You see? [*He looks very weary.*]

MADELEINE: You wait. You'll feel better, afterwards.

AMÉDÉE: You think so?

MADELEINE: Quick! Open the shutters!

AMÉDÉE: But they'll see us ...

[*Complete silence just at this moment.*]

MADELEINE: Do as I tell you ...

[AMÉDÉE *makes for the rear window and starts opening the shutters; he moves like a robot.*]

No one will see or hear you. There's a full moon ...

AMÉDÉE [*who has one shutter wide open*]: I can't believe this ... is me any more.

MADELEINE: The full moon blinds them all, dulls their brains, and sends them off into a deep sleep. They're all locked in their dreams.

AMÉDÉE: Think carefully, Madeleine, what you're making

me do. Think now! There'll be no turning back. We shall never, never see him again. You won't have any regrets or blame me for it, you won't start crying?

[AMÉDÉE *has opened the shutters wide; the cold light of the moon enters the room, merges with the green glow or even quells it.*]

MADELEINE: This is the ideal time. It's now or never; let's start.

AMÉDÉE [*gazing out of the window*]: How beautiful the night is!

MADELEINE: It's past midnight.

[*The cold and brilliant light is now flooding in through the window. The glowing sky can be seen outside exactly as* AMÉDÉE *describes it in his next speech. There is a striking contrast between the sinister room and the dazzling light effects. The mushrooms, which have not stopped growing and are now enormous, have silvery glints. The varied play of light seems to come not only from the window, but from all sides: through the walls and the cracks in the cupboard from the furniture and the mushrooms, big and small – the young ones sprouting on the floor are shining like glow-worms. The producer, the set-designer, and the lighting specialist should remember that although the atmosphere of the married couple's room has evidently changed slightly, it must definitely suggest the mingled presence of horror and beauty at the same time.*]

AMÉDÉE: Look, Madeleine . . . all the acacia trees are aglow. Their blossoms are bursting open and shooting up to the sky. The full-blown moon is flooding the Heavens with light, a *living* planet. The Milky Way is like creamy fire. Honeycombs, countless galaxies, comets' tails, celestial ribbons, rivers of molten silver, and brooks, lakes, and oceans of palpable light . . . [*He turns towards Madeleine, his hands outstretched.*] . . . There's some on my hand. Look, it's like velvet or lace . . .

[*Meanwhile* MADELEINE *is making the final preparations in the room; she is moving things about, an odd piece of furniture, making more room, trying in vain, and quickly giving up the attempt, to bend the dead man's legs a little.*]

... Light is silky ... I'd never touched it before ... [*He looks through the window again*] Sheaves of blossoming snow, trees in the sky, gardens and meadows ... domes and cupolas ... columns and temples ... [*Indicating the dead man regretfully*] He won't be able to see all this. [*At the window again*] And space, space, infinite space!

[*It is essential that all this should be said quite naturally, without exaggeration.*]

MADELEINE: Don't waste time. What's the matter with you? The night air's coming in. We shall both catch cold. Let's get started.

AMÉDÉE: But it's summer-time, Madeleine!

MADELEINE [*beginning to get excited*]: Is there anybody in the street?

AMÉDÉE: Nobody. Nothing stirring. Not a sound. It's deserted. [*To the dead man*] ... Poor old thing! ...

MADELEINE [*as the moment for carrying out their decision approaches and during the actual operation,* MADELEINE *gradually loses her calm and her self-control; it is* AMÉDÉE, *at the beginning and throughout, who remains, if not calm, at least detached from the proceedings, acting like a robot*]: This is hardly the time to feel sorry for him! [*What follows is accompanied by growing agitation on* MADELEINE'*s part.*] Come on, give me a hand, come al-o-ng!

[AMÉDÉE *leaves the window and walks towards Madeleine.*] Ssh! Listen! ... No, it's nothing. Come on, quickly!

AMÉDÉE: They can't see me, you said they were blinded by the moonlight ...

[*They are standing by the dead man;* AMÉDÉE *lifts his feet, then lets them fall back on the stool; he hardly knows where to begin.*]

MADELEINE [*almost wringing her hands*]: I know I did ... but you never can tell ... I only hope ... Come on, quickly ...

[*The intense activity of the following scenes can only be called feverish.* MADELEINE *looks at the clock, tries to move some furniture, and gives up; she shows all the signs of acute anxiety.*] Where are you going to dispose of the body?

AMÉDÉE: In the river, of course. Where else?

MADELEINE: Yes, in the river. [*Her hands pressed to her heart*] Have you any idea where?

[*It sounds as if someone is knocking at the right-hand door.*]

AMÉDÉE [*not frightened, because he is past fear*]: Someone's knocking.

MADELEINE [*hands still on her heart*]: No, It's the beating of my heart . . .

AMÉDÉE: If there really was someone knocking at the door, at this very moment it wouldn't be easy to tell the difference . . . Still, I don't suppose anyone will come . . .

[*The music could perhaps start again now. Strong regular beats –* MADELEINE'S *heart-beats seem to shake the whole set.* AMÉDÉE *is trying to drag the dead man by the feet: it looks remarkably difficult.* MADELEINE *helps him or tries to make more room by aimlessly pushing the furniture about. He interrupts his efforts to speak :*]

The most dangerous part, of course, is getting him from here to the river . . . still, it's only five hundred yards away. The first three hundred are the worst. Along our own street. The houses are tall on both sides. But . . . if I can move fast enough, while the moon's still casting its spell on the neighbours, I shan't be seen. Unless something awful happens and a piercing scream shatters their dreams and wakes them all up. Never mind! Nothing venture, nothing win. There's no alternative!

[MADELEINE *listens, growing steadily more frantic.*]

I've no choice.

MADELEINE [*helping* AMÉDÉE *to pull the feet*]: Come on, then, hurry up . . . hurry up . . .

AMÉDÉE: I'm doing my best! Stop nagging!

MADELEINE: I'm trying to help you, and you say I'm nagging! I'd like to know what you'd say if I left you to it!

[*In point of fact, each time* AMÉDÉE *manages to raise the feet a little and drag them, with much difficulty, a fraction nearer the window – twisting them round to avoid the right-hand door –*]

MADELEINE*impedes his progress, complicating his task, getting in his way and bringing his efforts to nought;* AMÉDÉE *is practically dragging Madeleine along with the dead body; he has become amazingly calm, a 'calm robot'.*]

MADELEINE: Pull harder . . .

[AMÉDÉE *makes a supreme, a superhuman effort. He pulls very hard: once, twice, a third time, and then, suddenly, the body yields to him, with a tremendous crash that breaks the silence, as chairs are pulled over, plaster falls from the ceiling, clouds of dust rise and the whole set trembles. This should give the impression that as the body – its head still invisible – is steadily pulled nearer the window, it is dragging the whole house with it and tugging at the entrails of the two principal characters.*]

MADELEINE [*shouting through the din*]: Be careful, or he'll have all the china down . . .

AMÉDÉE [*the same and still pulling*]: He'd really got rooted in the flat . . . He's so heavy . . . The strength of inertia!

MADELEINE [*as before*]: His head's not out of his room yet! Nor is his chest! Shall I go and pull him by the hair?

AMÉDÉE [*as before*]: Don't bother! . . . He's coming . . .
    [*The noise is reduced.*]
He's coming . . .

MADELEINE: That's it . . . Keep it up . . . Hurry up . . . The time's going . . . Pull . . . Tear him out . . .

AMÉDÉE [*backing towards the window, still pulling with all his might*]: He's harder to pull out than an old wisdom tooth . . . tougher than an oak . . .

MADELEINE: Wait. I'll come and help you. [*Help that hinders, that is pointless and confused.*] Oh, he's heavier than an oak . . . an oak made of iron with roots of lead . . .

AMÉDÉE [*has reached the rear window; he lays the feet on the window-ledge and stops to take breath and wipe his brow*]: Phew!

MADELEINE: Phew!

AMÉDÉE: And it's not over, yet. But we'll make it!

MADELEINE: It's specially important to be careful now. You're wet through already. So long as you don't catch cold . . .

[AMÉDÉE *prepares to resume his efforts.*]

Wait a moment. I'll have a look. [*She stands in the window beside the feet and looks down the street*] The street's still empty. We must watch out. I can't see any police on their beat.

AMÉDÉE: The streets *are* empty at this time of night.

MADELEINE: You mustn't throw him in the water where there are any barges; the moon doesn't affect bargees. Don't choose a place like that . . .

AMÉDÉE [*pointing through the window*]: I'll go a hundred yards farther up. It only means a little extra effort. Whatever I do, I can't help crossing little Torco Square, there, at the end of the street.

MADELEINE [*still looking through the window in the same direction*]: Can't you go another way? . . . That's a nuisance . . . right at the end there are lights in some of the windows . . . You might be spotted.

AMÉDÉE: That's the bar and brothel kept by the owner of our flat. It's used by American soldiers. You can see them sometimes walking about with their girls. There's not much risk. They don't know a word of the language . . . most of them! . . .

MADELEINE: Try and avoid them.

AMÉDÉE: That's not very easy. I'll have to chance it. It's a lovely night.

MADELEINE [*still looking through the window, her back to the audience; AMÉDÉE starts pulling the legs round in the middle of the stage; then goes back to the window*]: Amédée . . . I'm frightened . . . Oh dear . . . I suppose we must . . . We must . . . You'd better get on with it . . .

[*Standing at the window, AMÉDÉE pulls the body; it is obviously going much more easily; the clock strikes; the feet are over the window-sill and hang down the other side.*]

AMÉDÉE: He's rolling out, now . . . It's a lot easier . . . rolling out! [AMÉDÉE *is pulling at his legs, and the long, long body is winding out of the room, interminably; at each pull he rests it on the window-sill, while the long legs go sliding down, presumably to the pavement, and still issue, of course, incredibly long, slowly from the other room; the trunk has not appeared yet.*]

MADELEINE [*incoherently*]: I'm frightened . . . We shouldn't have made up our minds so quickly . . . We couldn't do anything else . . . We should have waited . . . No, we shouldn't have waited . . . It's all your fault . . . No, it's not your fault, I was right all the same, we simply had to . . .

[AMÉDÉE *goes on pulling; the body passes steadily over the window-sill.*]

Faster, pull faster, Amédée, I feel sick . . . You're killing me, Amédée, pull faster, there's no end to it, pull faster . . .

[*A loud noise comes from outside, from below;* AMÉDÉE *stops.*]

Oh! . . . Amédée, I told you to be careful . . . You seem to be doing it on purpose . . .

AMÉDÉE [*worried, all the same*]: What's happened?

MADELEINE: His feet, his feet! They've hit the pavement . . . You should do it more gently . . .

[AMÉDÉE *looks out of the window, too, next to Madeleine.*]

AMÉDÉE: I'm going down . . . Keep a good look-out . . .

MADELEINE: Am I to stay here all alone? . . . I'm frightened . . .

AMÉDÉE [*with one leg over the window-sill*]: What else can we do? It won't be for long. A few minutes and I'll be back!

[*He climbs out of the window; first only his head is visible, then his hands; finally he goes out of sight;* MADELEINE *watches him climb down.*]

MADELEINE: Be careful, dear, don't take risks, put your foot there . . . there . . . that's right . . . And now there . . . that's the way . . .

AMÉDÉE [*from below*]: All right . . .

MADELEINE: Are you down? Don't make too much noise.

AMÉDÉE [*from below*]: Can you see anyone?

MADELEINE [*through the window to Amédée*]: Can you see anyone?

AMÉDÉE [*from below*]: I can't see anyone.

MADELEINE [*through the window, to Amédée*]: Well, off you go, then ... Don't waste your time! ... Hurry up ... Pull ... Pull ...

[AMÉDÉE *pulls from the pavement below ... The same thing happens as previously, the rest of the legs appear, passing through the room and out of the window. These legs are surprisingly long, so it should last quite a long time; some strange muffled music could perhaps accompany this action. Meanwhile* MADELEINE *goes on encouraging her husband from the window:*]

Pull ... that's it ... again ... again ... pull ... there's still some more to come, pull ... pull ...

[*At last the trunk appears, and the enormous hands.*]

AMÉDÉE [*still in the street, pulling, he must have gone some distance already, almost as far as little Torco Square perhaps, with its bar and its brothel; his voice sounds a long way off*]: I've got to the square, Torco-o-o!

MADELEINE [*who has been gazing directly down at the pavement, has gradually raised her head and is now looking farther off*]: No. No-o-o! ... Go on pulling, there's more to come ... It's not finished yet ... Have you met a-anybo-ody?

AMÉDÉE: No-o-o-body! Don't be afraid! And you, have you? Can you see anyone?

MADELEINE: No-o one! Go on, pull ... pull ... pull! ...

[*She is still at the window, with her back to the audience; the body is still sliding out. Finally the shoulders appear, and then the head, which is so large that there is hardly room for it to pass through the doorway on the left; tremendously long white hair, an enormous white beard. When the head reaches the window, the long hair is still not quite out of the room.*]

Pull, Amédée ... pull ... Amé-é-edée ... pul-l-l ... pull ... pull ... Watch out for the barges ... Hurry up ... Don't catch cold ... Go straight there, don't hang abo-o-out ...

[*The head is right near the window; it should almost hide* MADELEINE.]

... Pul-l-l. ... Pul-l-l! ...

CURTAIN

ACT THREE

———◆◆◆———

Scene: little Torco Square. A few steps at the back, a small door, and one or two lighted windows, perhaps. This is the brothel-bar frequented by American soldiers. There is an indistinct hum coming from it; a jazz orchestra and men's and women's voices, but the sound should appear to come from farther off. The shadow of figures dancing could be seen behind the curtains, but not too much insistence should be laid on this; the shadows should pass once, rapidly, a fleeting vision. The music and the noise from the bar, which are only just audible in the theatre, will suddenly blare forth out of all proportion when, at a given moment, the door of the bar opens and an AMERICAN SOLDIER *is violently shoved outside; then the noise will fade again. Above the door and the window of the place there is a sign, which reads: 'BAR-MAISON DE TOLERANCE'. Near the steps, there might also be a lamp-post, between the door and the window. Above all no attempt should be made to make the set look like the traditional street-corner of low repute; it should not look like a tavern or a night-club; the walls of this brothel-bar are light in colour, it appears quite ordinary and respectable; the façade is fairly low; then a stretch of wall, which must not be too high to allow for the stage effect that is to come; the steps could be situated at one side of the bar-door, so that the latter is on a level with the stage; the houses to left and right are, on the other hand, tall and many-storeyed, with numerous windows. Above the wall of the brothel, an enormous moon, which lights the stage brilliantly. The entrance of* AMÉDÉE *will act as a signal for the light to intensify still further: huge clusters of stars will come into view, comets and shooting stars, fireworks in the sky.*

[*As the curtain rises on the third act the stage remains empty for a while. Music and muffled sounds from the bar. The windows of the other houses are dark and shuttered tight. Suddenly the bar-door is opened noisily; the music and the bar noises are incredibly loud while the door remains open, they might even come from several parts of the auditorium; a tall* AMERICAN SOLDIER *is being pushed vigorously by the shoulders out of the bar. From inside the bar can be heard:*]

VOICE OF THE OWNER OF THE BAR: No drunks in here! Get out!

[*Then the door slams behind the* AMERICAN SOLDIER, *the noise fades; the* SOLDIER *turns and bangs on the door.*]

SOLDIER! No! No! [*Banging on the door*] No . . . I'm not drunk . . . Open the door . . . I paid for it . . . [*Renewed banging*] Open the door . . . I wanna come in . . .

[*He knocks again. The door opens, and with a strong push the* SOLDIER *manages to force his way partly back; half in, half out, he appears to be fighting.*]

No! No! [*Then, yielding to superior force, he is almost completely outside again, except for one foot, which prevents the door from being shut tight*] I'm not drunk! I want some brandy! Cognac!

OWNER'S VOICE [*from within*]: Clear out! Don't you understand!

SOLDIER [*obstinately*]: I paid for it . . . I paid for it . . . I wan' Mado . . .

VOICE: Which Mado?

SOLDIER: I paid for it . . . I paid . . . for . . . Mado!

VOICE: Mado's a nice girl. She never goes with drunks. Mado . . . not for drunk men.

SOLDIER: I'm not . . . I'm not . . . I wan' . . . I . . . wan' . . . Mado!

[*A violent push from within sends the* SOLDIER *sprawling on the ground; the door closes.*]

SOLDIER [*sitting on the ground facing the bar and beating his fists rhythmically on the floor of the stage*]: Mado! Mado! Cognac! Mado! Cognac! Mado! Mado! Cognac!

[*The bar-door opens; the man's voice is heard:*]

VOICE: Shut your blasted trap or I'll call a policeman! A mil-it-ary pol-ice-man . . .

[*The door closes.*]

SOLDIER [*who has risen to his feet and hurled himself at the door — too late, the door shutting in his face — beats on it with his fists and shouts*]: Policeman!? Military Policeman!?... [*Then*] I am a Military Policeman! [*He turns and faces the audience, takes an armband bearing the letters M.P. from his pocket, fixes it on his arm, and says in a woebegone voice with his strong American accent*] Military Police, that's me! [*He shrugs his shoulders, makes a movement towards the door, hesitates, gives it up, and says, in a puzzled and disappointed tone*] Mado! Mado! [*Then, after scratching his head, he angrily rips off his M.P.'s armband, hurls it to the ground, takes a piece of chewing-gum from his pocket, and repeats, while he is chewing, in the same woe-begone voice*] Mado! Mado!

[*He sits down on the steps, still chewing, and falls asleep, his head dropping down between his long legs, which, in this position, come almost up to his shoulders; in the distance, the faint barking of a dog, then all is quiet, apart from the muffled music from the bar. Pause.* AMÉDÉE *comes in from the left, preceded by a noise not unlike that of a tin-can attached to a dog's tail; he is labouring under the weight of the dead body, which he is pulling after him feet first; he reaches the middle of the stage. Only the legs of the dead man can be seen, the rest of the body remaining in the wings; he drops the feet, which make a noise as they fall; he puffs and mops his brow for a moment.*]

AMÉDÉE: [*picks the feet up again and takes a step forward; noise of a tin-can; he stops; the tin-can again*] What's he up to, now! [*He pulls the feet very gently again and advances a little to the right; the tin-can is making less noise. He stops, once more out of breath*] Now I'm half-way there ... [*He looks round him*] I'm in luck ... The Square's empty. What a wonderful sky ... If only I hadn't this wretched job to do ... [*He picks up the feet again and progresses a little farther.*]

SOLDIER [*looming up out of the shadows, to* AMÉDÉE]: Do you speak English?

AMÉDÉE [*rather surprised*]: Oh, I'm sorry ...

SOLDIER: Did you see Mado?

AMÉDÉE: Madeleine, my wife?

SOLDIER: No, not Madeleine, Mado ... Do you know Mado?

AMÉDÉE [*struggling to speak English*]: Mado? . . . Mm? . . . I . . . do not . . . I . . . do . . . not . . . know . . . Mado . . .

SOLDIER: That's too bad!

AMÉDÉE: I beg your pardon? . . . What? . . .

SOLDIER [*noticing the body, without astonishment, as naturally as possible*]: Who's that? A friend? . . .

AMÉDÉE: I'm afraid I don't understand your language. Forgive me. Please don't keep me. I'm very busy.

SOLDIER [*indicating the body*]: A friend? A buddy of yours?

AMÉDÉE: Yes, yes, a friend . . . But it's none of your business. You're not a policeman . . . Ah! It's a great misfortune, the tragedy of our life . . . the skeleton in our cupboard . . . You wouldn't understand!

SOLDIER [*who really doesn't understand*]: Skeleton in your *what*? . . . I don't get it.

AMÉDÉE: I must go. I'm in a hurry. A great hurry. I don't like talking to people in the street. My wife has expressly forbidden me . . .

SOLDIER [*still not understanding*]: I see . . . I see . . .
[*He moves a few paces away.* AMÉDÉE *takes hold of the feet, pulls as hard as he can, makes little progress and stops, exhausted.*]

AMÉDÉE: I'll never do it, I'll never do it . . . And Madeleine's waiting for me . . . Oh dear . . . Perhaps I could leave him here . . . No, I can't leave him in the middle of the street . . . There'd be no room for the lorries to pass tomorrow; then there'd be an inquiry . . . they'd find out it comes from our place . . . and I'd be charged with obstructing the traffic on top of everything else . . . Oh, well! . . . Let's try again . . . [*He looks upwards for a second*] What a beautiful sky! [*Then*] Hardly the moment . . . Try again . . . Have a look at the sky when this is over . . . when this is over . . . [*He pulls, but unsuccessfully*] And I can't take him back to the flat either . . . it's no good, it's too much for me . . . I'm worn out . . .

SOLDIER: Wan' some help, bud?

AMÉDÉE: Please leave me alone, Monsieur, I don't want to be caught red-handed . . .

SOLDIER: No! . . . [*By gestures he makes Amédée understand that he wishes to help him.*]

AMÉDÉE: Well, of course . . . If you really want to . . . thank you . . . it's most kind of you, it will be much quicker . . . I have to be back as soon as possible to finish my play . . .

SOLDIER: Play?

[AMÉDÉE *shows him by sign language that he writes.*]

SOLDIER: You . . . a writer? Gee! That's swell! You're . . . writin' a play?

AMÉDÉE: Yes. A play in which I'm on the side of the living against the dead. One of Madeleine's ideas. I'm all for taking sides, Monsieur, I believe in progress. It's a problem play attacking nihilism and announcing a new form of humanism, more enlightened than the old.

SOLDIER [*who still cannot understand*]: I get it . . . I get it . . .

[*With these words the* SOLDIER *gives a tremendous pull with all his strength: a great part of the body is pulled into a heap upon the stage; the arms can be seen emerging from it and, on the left, the shoulders and the beginning of the neck. But the pull has doubtless been too strong, for it has made a terrific noise and Madeleine's voice can be heard faintly from far away.*]

MADELEINE'S VOICE: Amédée . . . What are you doing?

AMÉDÉE [*scared*]: There's that Madeleine again! Always fussing . . . [*To the Soldier*] Please . . . not so hard . . . Oh dear, oh dear . . . Someone's sure to have heard . . .

[*The noise has indeed started the dogs barking and set the trains in motion: they can be heard rolling along in the distance, quietly at first, much more loudly later on. Desperately:*]

What have you done, Monsieur? You've made the dogs bark and started all the trains . . .

SOLDIER: Huh! [*Understanding*] Ah, yea, dawgs . . . I get it . . . wuff! wuff! wuff! yea . . . yea . . .

[*He seems amused by this:* AMÉDÉE *barks too, to make sure he understands he means dogs. Seeing no reason for alarm and unaware of Amédée's fright, the* AMERICAN *suddenly puts his finger to his brow, like someone who has a brilliant idea; then,*] *taking hold of Amédée by the shoulders, he spins him round like a top.*]

AMÉDÉE [*unable to resist*]: But ... please ... I say ... look here ... [*As he realizes that the body is rolling up round his waist, he begins to spin round under his own steam so that the body shall go on rolling round him*] Yes, thank you, that's an excellent idea ... Americans are really quite intelligent ... that's fine ...

SOLDIER [*pleased to see that Amédée has understood, moves aside a little to let him continue unaided*]: Good, eh?

AMÉDÉE: It's much easier ... I should have thought of it before ... excellent idea ... [*He stops spinning round for a moment*] Now it's my turn to do you a favour. If ever you want to learn French, never use the sound *u* in conversation. The *u* is dangerous, it's a sharp, pointed sound. English is a soft tongue, not dangerous at all. There's no *u* in it, as there is in French.

SOLDIER: I get it ... I get it ...

AMÉDÉE: *U*, it's like a knife, an angle, the point of a needle, beware of it, beware ... *u* is a whistling sound ... If you can't avoid saying an *u*, you must round your lips into a circle, like this, to stop it escaping. Beware of cuts or grazes, of anything that penetrates or dislocates or pierces ...

SOLDIER: I get it ... I get it ...

AMÉDÉE: ... a cutting wit slips its barb slyly into conversation ... Are you a geometrician?

SOLDIER: I get it ... I get it ...

AMÉDÉE: In that case put yourself on the side of the spheres ... Choose a curve and not an angle, a circle not a triangle, an ellipse but never a parallelepiped ... cylinders, perhaps, but cones only now and then ... never pyramids as the Egyptians did, that's what caused their downfall ...

SOLDIER: I get it ... I get it ...

AMÉDÉE: And above all, evade the question ... always move in a circle and paraphrase and paraphrase ... I paraphrase ... you paraphrase ... we paraphrase ... keep

going round and round or you'll have to stick to the
point . . .

[*While saying these last words* AMÉDÉE *has started spinning
round again, rolling the body round and round his waist as he does
so, without a word now and growing steadily more anxious; for
this procedure is accompanied by a continuous and penetrating
whistle. But it is too late to stop, he must go on whatever happens.
In the end the whole district is astir; in the sky there is a
renewed outbreak of shooting stars, fireworks, etc.; shutters
are thrown open; windows light up and heads appear at
every floor. The bar-door opens and the owner appears on
the threshold, accompanied by a girl,* MADO, *and a* SECOND
AMERICAN SOLDIER. *Meanwhile* AMÉDÉE *goes on
spinning round, with the body coiling round him, and the noise
of the trains and the barking of the dogs growing louder and
louder.*]

BAR-OWNER: But the trains shouldn't have started yet!

FIRST SOLDIER [*catching sight of Mado*]: Mado! Mado!
Gee, what a surprise! [*And seeing the Second Soldier*] Hi,
Bob!

[*The* FIRST SOLDIER *goes towards Mado and the Second
Soldier, who has advanced a few steps forward; he shakes them
by the hand, kisses Mado and is delighted to have found her
again.*]

SECOND SOLDIER: Hiya, Harry!

MADO [*to the First Soldier*]: Hallo, you. Are you the one they
chucked out?

FIRST SOLDIER: Uuh?

SECOND SOLDIER [*to the First*]: She wants to know if you're
the one they threw out?

FIRST SOLDIER [*jubilantly, to Mado*]: Oh, yeah, that was me
. . . threw me out . . . [*Pointing to the Owner*] That guy over
there . . .

[*He lifts Mado into his arms.*]

BAR-OWNER [*from the doorway, to Amédée*]: You've found a
funny job for yourself! . . . Why, it's that old tenant of mine
. . . it's M. Amédée . . .

97

[*The latter is still turning, but not so easily; he is tangled up in dead man's long legs.*]

... Playing a game like that, at your age! ... How's the wife?

[*Someone is blowing a whistle off-stage.*]

It's the cops!

AMÉDÉE [*standing quite still, petrified*]: Hell! The police!

[TWO POLICEMEN *do, in fact, now come on at the double, blowing their whistles.*]

MADO [*to the two Americans, who are looking rather scared*]: It's not for us ...

FIRST POLICEMAN [*acknowledging them as he passes*]: Evening ...

[AMÉDÉE *turns to flee homewards, to the left, still entangled.*]

A MAN [*at a window*]: Julie ... come and look!

[*The* POLICEMEN *run off left after Amédée, who has disappeared.*]

SECOND SOLDIER [*explaining the situation to his friends*]: That's a buddy of his!

[AMÉDÉE *reappears from the left and vanishes behind the low wall at the rear, behind the bar. Shouts of laughter from the windows.*]

MADO: A pal of his? What's he doing with him, then?

BAR-OWNER [*hands in pockets*]: Now you're asking!

[*The* TWO POLICEMEN *reappear from the left.*]

FIRST POLICEMAN: Where did he go?

SECOND POLICEMAN: Where did he go?

BAR-OWNER [*pointing to a part of the body lying on the stage*]: That's a piece of the incriminating corpse.

[*Laughter from* MADO *and the* AMERICANS.]

A WOMAN [*at her window*]: That way, officers, he must be behind the wall! ...

FIRST POLICEMAN [*looking at the body*]: Is that really the corpse?

SECOND POLICEMAN: Never mind that ... Let's catch him first!

[*They run after Amédée and disappear behind the wall.*]

BAR-OWNER [*to himself*]: Well, M. Amédée! You're a fine one! I'd never have thought it!

A WOMAN [*at a window*]: They won't catch him!

A MAN [*at a window*]: They will!

A WOMAN [*at a window*]: No, they won't!

A MAN [*at a window*]: Yes, they will! [*To his wife, who is inside*] Come and look, Julie! . . . There's no charge. Hurry and get up!

    [*Flashes of light, stars, fireworks.*]

MADO: Ooh! Fireworks!

BAR-OWNER [*with a shrug of his shoulders*]: They're not. They're stars . . .

A WOMAN [*at a window, to her husband, who is inside*]: They won't catch him, you know . . . [*To the gentleman at the other window*] They won't, will they, Monsieur?

MAN [*at the window*]: Want a bet on it?

FIRST SOLDIER [*to Mado*]: I'll take you along . . .

MADO: All right with me . . . To America!

FIRST POLICEMAN [*from behind the wall, where he is invisible*]: Catch him!

SECOND SOLDIER [*to Mado*]: Yeah . . . to the United States of America . . .

    [*Suddenly a surprising thing happens. The body wound round Amédée's waist seems to have opened out like a sail or a huge parachute; the dead man's head has become a sort of glowing banner, and* AMÉDÉE's *head can be seen appearing above the rear wall, drawn up by the parachute; then his shoulders, his trunk, and his legs follow.* AMÉDÉE *is flying up out of reach of the policeman. The banner is like a huge scarf, on which the head of the dead man is drawn, recognizable by the long beard, etc.*]

FIRST POLICEMAN [*behind the wall*]: Catch him, catch him . . . He's getting away from us . . .

AMÉDÉE [*in flight*]: Please forgive me, Ladies and Gentlemen, it's not my fault, I can't help it, it's the wind . . . Really, it's not me.

A MAN [*at a window*]: Don't often see anything like this . . .

A WOMAN [*at a window*]: He's flying away! He says he doesn't
want to, but he looks quite pleased all the same.

SECOND POLICEMAN [*jumping up from behind the wall; a hand
appears, catching hold of Amédée's shoe, then disappears again*]:
Bastard!

[*The* BAR-OWNER, MADO, *and the* TWO SOLDIERS *run
into the centre of the stage, where they can watch Amédée flying
away.*]

BAR-OWNER:
MADO: } Oooh!
SOLDIERS:

[*The* AMERICANS, *naturally, pronounce this sound with a
strong American accent. The* SECOND SOLDIER *quickly takes
out a camera and tries to take a picture of Amédée in flight.*]

SECOND POLICEMAN [*behind the wall*]: All I caught was his
shoe!

MADO [*to the Second American Soldier*]: You'll give me a snap,
won't you?

WOMAN [*at the window*]: I said they wouldn't catch him!

FIRST SOLDIER [*bursting with excitement and throwing his cap
into the air, as the* TWO POLICEMEN *re-appear, looking rather
crestfallen*]: Hiya, boy! Hip! Hip! Hooray!

MADO *and* THE PEOPLE AT THE WINDOWS [*watching
AMÉDÉE fly slowly away*]: Oooh!

BAR-OWNER: That's what I call an escape!

FIRST SOLDIER: Attaboy! Yippee! [*He is jumping about with
excitement.*]

[*The* SECOND SOLDIER *has finished taking his photographs;
from the windows and from all sides of the stage, applause rings
out:*]

Hip! Hip! Hooray!

[*One of the* POLICEMEN *is holding Amédée's shoe.*]

MADO *and* THE AMERICANS: Hip! Hip! Hooray!

THE PEOPLE AT THE WINDOWS: Hip! Hip! Hooray!

ALL TOGETHER [*except the two policemen*]: Hip! Hip! Hooray!

FIRST POLICEMAN [*blowing his whistle*]: Move along there!
Move along!

[MADELEINE *appears from the left, her hair unkempt, looking quite distracted.*]

MADELEINE [*running to the centre of the stage*]: Amédée! ... Amédée! ... Have you seen Amédée? What's happened to Amédée?

SECOND POLICEMAN: Is that your husband, Madame?

MADELEINE [*looking up into the sky*]: Heavens! It can't be! It's incredible! Is that really him?

FIRST POLICEMAN: Well, Madame, I'm afraid it is ... Fine state of affairs!

MADELEINE [*looking into the sky*]: Amédée! Amédée! Amédée! Come down, Amédée, you'll catch a chill, you'll catch cold!

SECOND POLICEMAN: Amédée! Amédée! Come down, M. Amédée! Your wife's calling you!

ALL TOGETHER: Amédée! Amédée! Amédée!

[*More bursts of hilarity from the windows.* AMÉDÉE *re-appears still in mid-air, on another side of the stage; everyone rushes over.*]

MAN [*at the window*]: Hey ... there ... Jack-in-the-box! [*To the Policeman*] And you there, leave him alone, can't you! Down with the police!

AMÉDÉE: I'm terribly sorry. Please forgive me, Ladies and Gentlemen ... Please don't think ... I should like to stay ... stay with my feet on the ground ... It's against my will ... I don't want to get carried away ... I'm all for progress, I like to be of use to my fellow men ... I believe in social realism ...

WOMAN [*at the window*]: He's a good talker.

MAN [*at the window, to his wife inside*]: He's making a speech ...

AMÉDÉE: I swear to you that I'm all against dissolution ... I stand for immanence, I'm against transcendence ... yet I wanted, I wanted to take the weight of the world on my shoulders ... I apologize, Ladies 'n Gentlemen, I apologize profusely.

MADELEINE: Come down, Amédée, I'll arrange things with the police ... [*To the Policemen*] It *will* be all right, won't it?

FIRST POLICEMAN: Why yes, Madame, of course, we'll fix it all up. . . .

MADELEINE: Amédée, you can come home, the mushrooms have bloomed . . . the mushrooms have bloomed . . .

ALL TOGETHER [*except for* AMÉDÉE]: The mushrooms have bloomed . . .

FIRST SOLDIER: Hey what are they talking about?

MAN [*at the window, to his wife inside*]: It's all about some mushrooms . . .

WOMAN [*at the window, to her husband inside*]: They're mushroom-growers . . .

AMÉDÉE: Madeleine, I promise you, you can really believe me . . . I didn't want to run away from my responsibilities . . . It's the wind, *I* didn't do anything! . . . It's not on purpose! . . . Not of my own free will!

WOMAN [*at the window, to the Man at the other window*]: It's not his fault, if it's not of his own free will . . .

> [AMÉDÉE *is going up, throwing down kisses as fast as he can, and says:*]

AMÉDÉE: Forgive me, Ladies and Gentlemen, I'm terribly sorry! Forgive me! [*Then*] Oh, dear! But I feel so frisky, so frisky. [*He disappears.*]

WOMAN [*at the window*]: It's a course of rejuvenation.

FIRST POLICEMAN: You might at least drop us the other shoe!

MADELEINE [*wringing her hands*]: Amédée! . . . Amédée! . . . Your career in the theatre!

MADO: Why don't you let him alone, Madame . . .

FIRST SOLDIER [*to Madeleine*]: Off he goes . . .

MADELEINE: Amédée, Amédée, you'll make yourself ill, you haven't taken your mackintosh . . . [*Noticing the BAR-OWNER*] Oh, good evening, Monsieur, I hadn't seen you there before! [*Then*] Amédée!

MADO: He's going to vanish into the Milky Way!

> [AMÉDÉE'S *second shoe falls on the stage from above.*]

SECOND POLICEMAN [*picking it up*]: Well, that's very thoughtful!

FIRST POLICEMAN [*to the second*]: That makes us one each!
[*They share the shoes out; then his jacket falls, and a number of cigarettes; the* POLICEMEN *rush for them, share them out between themselves and light up.*]

WOMAN [*at the window*]: He's not what you'd call stingy!

MAN [*at the window*]: Of course, it's the police that get the benefit!

WOMAN [*at the window*]: It's always the same!
[*The* POLICEMEN *offer cigarettes all round and throw them up to the people at the windows.*]

MAN [*at the window, catching one*]: Thank you, Officer.

WOMAN [*at the window, as above*]: Thank you, Officer. [*To her husband inside*] Here you are: cigarettes!

MADELEINE [*gazing up at the sky, which is brilliantly lit*]: Come along, Amédée, won't you ever be serious? You may have gone up in the world, but you're not going up in *my* estimation!

FIRST POLICEMAN [*looking up at the sky and wagging his finger at Amédée, as one would at a child*]: You little rascal, you! Little rascal!

ALL TOGETHER [*imitating the Policeman's gesture*]: Little rascal! Little rascal!

FIRST SOLDIER: Why, Junior, you bad boy!

MADO: He's out of sight. Completely disappeared!
[*Brilliant flashes. Blazing lights from all sides.*]

BAR-OWNER: Why don't you all come and have a drink!

FIRST POLICEMAN: Why not?

MADELEINE: Oh, no! . . . I . . . don't know if I ought to . . . I'm not thirsty!

MADO: Don't worry about it, Madame. It was the wind that did it. Men are all alike. When they don't need you any more, they leave you in the lurch! . . . Yours is nothing but a great big baby!

WOMAN [*at the window*]: He won't come back to you, Madame.

MAN [*at the window*]: He *may* come back to you . . .

WOMAN [*at the window*]: Oh, no! He won't come back.

Exactly the same thing happened to me with my first husband. I never saw him again.

MADELEINE: I shall be all alone now. I don't want to marry again! And to think he never finished his play!

SECOND POLICEMAN [*gently pushing Madeleine*]: Oh ... People always say that ... You never know ... People forget ... Why don't you come? ... After all, the drinks are on the house ...

MADELEINE [*moving towards the bar with all the others*]: It's such a pity! He was quite a genius, you know, really!

BAR-OWNER: All that talent wasted! It's a bad day for literature!

MADO: No one is indispensable!

[*They all go into the bar.*]

MAN [*at the window, to his wife inside*]: And *now, we* can go to bed ... We've got to be up early tomorrow! ... Come on, Julie ...

WOMAN [*at the window*]: Let's close the shutter, Eugène, the show's over!

CURTAIN

August 1953

This is another ending to the play, which takes staging problems into account; it is easier to produce and replaces Act III, the curtain never falling at the end of Act II.

The change of scene is no longer indicated by a change of set, but by the intrusion of fresh characters on to the stage, and (at the Théâtre de Babylone) by a scenic device allowing the rear wall only of the dining-room to disappear, so that the action passes in an ill-defined space, glowing with light.

MADELEINE: Pull ... pul-l-l ... Why don't you pull ... ?

AMÉDÉE [*from far off, invisible*]: I'm pul-ling ... it's not coming very easily ... what's the matter with it ...

MADELEINE [*cupping her hands*]: But pul-l-l ... you've only got to pull harder ... Amédée ... come on ... pul-l-l ...

pul-l-l . . . as har-ard . . . as you ca-an! You're not pulling as hard as you ca-an!

AMÉDÉE [*as before*]: I'm do-o-ing . . . my-y . . . be-est . . .

MADELEINE [*as before*]: Put some stre-ength into it! . . . Why don't you ma-ake an effort . . . Don't be so l-a-azy! . . . [*Pause.*] Th-a-t's better!

AMÉDÉE [*as before*]: Is there – still – a lot m-o-ore? M-o-ore?

MADELEINE [*as before*]: Only the h-e-ad!

[MADELEINE *is still at the window, which is almost completely blocked; there is just enough room for her to show her head.*]

AMÉDÉE [*as before*]: I've adva-anced a little . . . I must stop to get my brea-th! . . .

MADELEINE [*as before*]: There's no time to l-o-ose! You must be m-a-ad . . . There's no t-i-i-me . . . you must p-u-l-l . . . pu-l-l . . . Hurry u-u-up . . . The night is sh-o-ort . . . it'll soon be d-a-y! . . .

AMÉDÉE [*as before*]: Just a second, only a second . . . Then I'll have more str-ength . . . I must r-e-st . . .

MADELEINE [*as before*]: You can rest l-a-ter . . . There's no t-i . . . ime! Pul-l-l . . . your h-e-a-rt's not in it! . . .

AMÉDÉE [*as before*]: All r-i-ght . . . I'm pu-lling . . . you must p-u-ush to-o-o . . .

MADELEINE [*to herself*]: Can't do a thing by himself! [*She pushes the head outwards, towards Amédée*] Pu-l-l . . . That's right . . . That's it . . .

AMÉDÉE [*as before*]: Is there any m-o-re! . . . P-u-ush . . . p-u-ush!

MADELEINE [*as before*]: Only the h-e-ad! . . . Where a-a-r-e you?

AMÉDÉE [*as before*]: At the other side of the sq-u-a-re!

MADELEINE [*cupping her hands*]: Go o-on . . . go o-on! . . . once ag-a-ain . . . ! Be c-a-areful! Don't pull the window out!

[*A violent jolt.*]

Not so h-a-ard!

[*The walls shake.*]

Not so h-a-ard, I tell you . . . Can you hear m-e-e? You'll have the whole h-o-use d-o-o-own . . .!

[*The whole set trembles violently.*]

We'll never be able to pay the o-w-ner compens-a-ation . . . be c-a-areful! Don't be so r-o-u-gh! L-i-sten to me, you br-u-te! . . . Do you h-e-ar!

[*The head disappears.*]

That's it! That's it! It's out! [*To Amédée*] It's o-o-u-t! [*A rapid glance round the empty room*] We shall have to get some furniture now, to furnish the flat!

[*The head has disappeared completely from view through the now empty window-frame.*]

Get on the w-a-y! The worst is o-over! And come back so-o-on! Hurry up . . . what-ever you d-o-o . . . hu-rr-y . . . there's w-o-rk to be d-o-one! . . . [*She gazes into the distance, shielding her eyes with her hand*] Amédée! Amédée! Hey! Amédée! A-a-answer me! Let me kn-o-ow how you're getting o-o-on!

[*While* MADELEINE *is calling, watching and getting in a state,* MADO *and the* AMERICAN SOLDIER *appear behind her. Dance music.*]

MADO [*wheedling*]: If you teach me American, I teach you French . . .

SOLDIER: I get it . . . I get it . . . O.K. . . . O.K.!

[MADELEINE *goes on making signs from the window.*]

MADO [*to the* SOLDIER]: You speak French?

SOLDIER: Parlez-vous anglais? . . . Je . . . parle . . . français. Mademoiselle, Madame, Monsieur.

MADO [*to the soldier, wantonly*]: We have good time together, you see!

MADELEINE [*as before*]: Amédée! Amédée! Amé-éd-dée!

[*While* MADO *and the* SOLDIER *are flirting, they could come up to the window on either side of Madeleine, as though she did not exist; they talk to each other over her head and even push her lightly aside at times in order to touch each other.*]

MADO [*to the* SOLDIER]: You speak well French?

SOLDIER: Un peu – beaucoup – passionnément.

MADO [*simpering wantonly*]: You liar ... American liar! ...

MADELEINE [*shouting through cupped hands*]: Amédée! ... A-a-answer me! ... Where a-a-are you? [*To the Soldier*] Have you any binoculars?

SOLDIER: Uuh?

MADO [*to the Soldier*]: She ask you glasses ...

SOLDIER: Oh, field-glasses. O.K.! [*He hands the field-glasses to* MADELEINE, *who looks through them into the distance; to Mado*] Hey, vous parlez anglais bien!

MADO [*to the Soldier*]: A leetle ... you goddam son-of-a-bitch!

MADELEINE [*with the glasses*]: I can see you ... Amédée ... What are you doing down there ... You're going the wrong way!

SOLDIER [*to Mado*]: You're a cute little baby!
[*Stretching his hand over Madeleine, he caresses Mado's breasts.*]

MADELEINE: [*with the glasses*] Go round the corner, Amédée! What a silly idiot! Cross the road! Don't drop him, whatever you do!

SOLDIER [*caressing Mado*]: What's the French for these? Pamplemousse?

MADO [*giggling*]: Grapefruit! ... is like lemon!

MADELEINE [*with the glasses*]: Well, cro-o-oss it! There aren't any cars about now. The road's clear! What are you w-a-i-ting for!

MADO [*to Madeleine*]: Oh, must you shout so loud? I can't hear what he's saying! Can't hear ourselves speak!

MADELEINE [*to Mado*]: He's taken the wrong road! [*With the glasses, shouting into the distance*] ... Amédée ... do you hear me? Amédée! ...

SOLDIER [*to Mado, still caressing her breasts*]: Lemon or melon?

MADO [*to the Soldier*]: I do not mind ... just as you like ... [*Simpering wantonly:*] If you satisfied ... chéri!

SOLDIER: Lemons grow on melon-trees!
[*He kisses Mado. They have now taken up almost all the room at the window; Madeleine is flattened in a corner with her glasses.*]

MADO: Et vice versa!

MADELEINE [*as before*]: Amédée! Amédée! Amé-é-dée!

MADO [*in the Soldier's arms*]: Darling!

SOLDIER: Baby! [MADO *and the* SOLDIER *move slightly away from the window, executing vague dance-steps; they stand still, then move off again; and so they continue almost until the end of the play.*] Lemon! Melon! Melon! Lemon!

MADELEINE [*as before*]: Look out for the curb, Amédée, and what-e-ever you do, do-o-on't trip up! Don't go near the lamp-post or you'll both be se-e-en!

SOLDIER [*petting the girl*]: And these? Pommes? Poires?

MADELEINE [*as before*]: Keep *away* from the *light*, Am-é-dée! ...

MADO: Apples and pears?

MADELEINE [*as before*]: Don't make any n-o-i-se, Am-é-é-édée! Take the sh-o-rt c-u-t! The sh-o-rt c-u-t!

MADO [*to Madeleine, who does not hear her*]: Oh *really*, Madame! Not so *loud*!

MADELEINE [*as before*]: Cross! ... Turn the c-o-rner!

SOLDIER [*to Mado*]: Up those stairs!

MADO: Coucou! Coucou!

MADELEINE [*as before*]: Cross ... turn ... cross ... t-u-r-n ...

SOLDIER [*to Mado*]: Cuckoo! Cuckoo!

SOLDIER AND MADO: Cuc...koo...cou...cou...cuc ...koo...cou...cou...

MADELEINE [*as before*]: Roll him round you ... You've only got to roll him up! He'll be easier to carry! I have to teach you everything! ... And you're not a child! [*To Mado and the Soldier*] He has to be told everything! [*To Amédée*] Well, roll him round you, then ... r-o-l-l him!

MADO [*to the Soldier*]: Gibraltar!

SOLDIER: Casablanca!

MADELEINE: He's so awkward ... He's turned the corner ... what on earth can he be doing now!

SOLDIER [*still to Mado*]: Zanzibar!

MADO: Timbuctoo!

MADELEINE: What *can* he be doing! He must be wool-gathering!

SOLDIER: And these? Poppies?

MADO: Puppies?

MADELEINE [*to the other two, who pay no attention*]: He must have met someone! He'll be gossiping! And I told him not to! If you only knew how impossible he is!

SOLDIER [*to Mado*]: Puppy dogs' tails!

MADO: Ah yes! Chiens, toutous, dogs!

MADELEINE: Oh dear, oh dear, oh dear! [*She walks about the stage in great agitation*] He must be resting at every tree!

SOLDIER: That's what little boys are made of!

MADELEINE [*as above*]: I'd better go and see! [*She puts on her hat*] I can't leave the silly fool all alone; after all, he *is* my husband!

MADO: You're a wolf!

SOLDIER: There's a wolf around!

MADELEINE [*hat on head*]: He's a lazy hound! Oh dear, oh dear, oh dear!

SOLDIER: A wolf . . . Aouh! aouh! aouh! aouh!

MADO *and the* SOLDIER [*holding hands*]: Aouh! Aouh! Aouh! Aouh! Brrr! Aouh!

MADELEINE: He can't do a thing properly, when he's by himself!

[*While* MADO *and the* SOLDIER *go on yapping amorously at each other, a loud noise like a tin-can rattling is suddenly heard coming from Amédée's direction. Vehemently, much distressed:*] Ah! He's fallen down! I knew he would! I was sure of it! I should never have let him have his own way! I was quite right to try and stop him! Oh dear, oh dear! [*Into the wings*] Get up again! !

[*Sound of a tin-can once more; furious barking breaks out in the distance.* MADO *and the* SOLDIER *go on with their little game.*] He'll wake everybody up! He'll be seen! Where is he? What'll people say! We're ruined! It's his fault! I knew this would happen!

[*Noise of trains starting. Little trains can be seen moving in the background.*]

Now he's started up the trains! [*She returns to the window.*] Come back, Amédée! Don't leave me all alone!

[*A* MAN's *head appears at a window on one side of the stage, or emerges from the orchestra pit.*]

MAN: What's up? It's not time for the trains yet!

MADELEINE: Where are you? Come qui-i-ckly! Bring him back with you! Don't leave him in the road, he'll block the traffic! Stop star-gazing!

MAN: Making me lose my sleep! I'm a working man!

[*Whistles are being blown.*]

MADELEINE: My God, the police!

SOLDIER: Police?

MADO: Don't worry, it's not for us!

MADELEINE: There he is, running! Quick! Drop him in the road! He won't, of course, he's stubborn as a mule!

MAN: Julie . . . get up, come and look!

[*A* WOMAN's *head appears next to the Man's.*]

WOMAN: What's up? The police?

MAN: It's M. Amédée! Funny sort of state he's in!

MADO [*to Soldier*]: Come and see!

MADELEINE: Make a dash for it!

WOMAN: The cops are after him! [*Confused din in the distance; policemen's whistles.*] He's running quite fast for his age!

MADELEINE: Don't da-w-dle!

MADO [*to the Soldier*]: You like to see what happens in the streets?

SOLDIER: Les rues de Paris!

WOMAN: What have they been up to now?

MAN: Can't tell, with people like that!

MADELEINE: Don't fall o-over! Run, can't you?

MAN: He's tearing across the square!

MADELEINE: Look out for the traffic lights!

SOLDIER: Oh boy, oh boy!

MAN: It's a bit of a handicap . . . a parcel like that!

MADO: They won't catch him!

WOMAN: Yes, the police'll have him!

MADO: I tell you they won't!

MADELEINE: He's round the corner! With a dog at his heels! It'll rip his trousers!!

WOMAN: He's gone round the corner, Officer! After him!

MADO: Mind your own business!

MADELEINE: I can't see him now!

WOMAN: Behind the wall, Officer!

MAN: Don't interfere!

FIRST POLICEMAN [*the upper part of his body only appearing, a whistle in his hand*]: Move along there!

MADELEINE: Do you hear, Amédée? Move a bit faster!

MAN: Home sweet home!

SOLDIER: Where is he?

MADO: Down there, at the corner!

MAN: They won't catch him!

SOLDIER: What a champ! Attaboy!

MADO: No!

MADELEINE [*wringing her hands*]: It's my husband! It's my husband!

WOMAN: Yes!

MAN [*to Woman*]: You keep out of this!

WOMAN: She says it's her husband! Why don't they keep to themselves?

POLICEMAN: Move along!

WOMAN: That way! That way!

MAN: He's got the body with him!

MADELEINE [*running about wildly*]: Drop the corpse!

POLICEMAN: Where's he gone?

[AMÉDÉE *runs on from the back; with the dead man's hat on his head and the beard on his face.*]

WOMAN: There he goes!

MADO: There he goes!

MADELEINE: So there you are! It's about time!

[*The* SECOND POLICEMAN *appears at the back.*]

AMÉDÉE: Don't lose your head!

FIRST POLICEMAN [*to* SECOND POLICEMAN]: Don't let him get away! Catch him!

WOMAN: Catch him!

MAN: They won't have him!

SOLDIER: Attaboy!

[*The* SECOND POLICEMAN *tries to lay hands on Amédée;
the* FIRST POLICEMAN *also stretches out his hand from the
orchestra pit, in an attempt to catch him; but it is all in vain.*
AMÉDÉE *is suddenly lifted from the ground and begins to fly.*]

FIRST POLICEMAN [*who has caught nothing but Amédée's shoe*]:
The bastard!

MAN:
WOMAN:
MADO: } Ooh!
SOLDIER:

MADELEINE: Stop doing that, Amédée! Who told you to do
that?

SECOND POLICEMAN: He's getting away!

MAN [*to Woman*]: I told you they wouldn't catch him!

MADO: Marvellous!

SOLDIER [*enthusiastically*]: Oh boy, oh boy!

AMÉDÉE [*flying away*]: I'm not doing it on purpose,
Madeleine! I can't help myself!

FIRST POLICEMAN: All I caught is his left shoe!

MADELEINE: Oh yes, you can, you're doing it on purpose!

AMÉDÉE [*flying away*]: I promise you, Madeleine, it's not my
fault, it's the wind!

MADO: You see, he says it's the wind!

MAN: It's the wind!

SOLDIER: Attaboy!

WOMAN: It's not the wind!

FIRST POLICEMAN [*shoe in hand, to Madeleine severely*]: Is that
your husband, Madame?

MADELEINE: Yes, officer, I'm afraid it is!

AMÉDÉE [*slowly rising*]: It's not my fault! I hope you'll all
forgive me!

SECOND POLICEMAN [*to Madeleine*]: Tell him to come
down! At once!

MADELEINE: Come down at once!

MADO [*to Madeleine*]: Why don't you leave him alone!

AMÉDÉE [*still hanging in mid air*]: I swear it's not my fault, please forgive me, all of you, it's the wind that did it! I couldn't help myself!

MAN: Don't often see anything like this!

WOMAN: He's flying away! He says he doesn't want to, but he looks happy enough!

MADELEINE [*to Amédée*]: Will you come down at once! Do as everyone tells you!

[*The* SOLDIER *takes out a camera and photographs Amédée flying away.*]

SECOND POLICEMAN: A fine thing! Respectable people too!

MADO [*to the Soldier*]: I say, you give me one, yes?

FIRST POLICEMAN: Hi, you there! It's forbidden to take photographs!

MADELEINE: Amédée! Just you come down! You'll catch cold!

SECOND POLICEMAN: Come down, M. Amédée, your wife wants you!

MAN: Hallo, there . . . Jack-in-the-box! [*To the Policeman*] Come off it! Down with the police!

WOMAN [*to Man*]: Aren't you ashamed of yourself?

AMÉDÉE [*in mid air*]: I don't know what to say, please forgive me, Ladies and Gentlemen; you mustn't think . . . I should like to keep my feet on the ground . . . It's against my will . . . I don't want to get carried away . . . I should like to be of some use to my fellow men . . . I believe every man should realize his limitations . . .

MADO: Oh! He knows how to talk!

SOLDIER: Yippee! Yippee!

MAN: He's making a speech!

AMÉDÉE [*as above*]: I swear to you I'm against dissolution . . . I stand for immanence, I'm against transcendence! I'm terribly sorry . . . Please accept my apologies! . . .

MADELEINE: Listen to me, Amédée, and come down . . . I'll make it all right with the police! . . . [*To the Policemen*] Won't I?

FIRST POLICEMAN: Why yes, of course, Madame. It can all be arranged! . . .

MADELEINE: Amédée, you can come home now, the mushrooms have bloomed . . .

SOLDIER: I don't get it!

MAN: It's all about some mushrooms!

WOMAN: They're mushroom growers!

AMÉDÉE [*in mid air*]: Madeleine, I promise you, you can really believe me this time, I didn't want to run away from my responsibilities . . . It's the wind, I didn't do it on purpose, not of my own free will!

MADO: It's not his fault, if it's not of his own free will!

AMÉDÉE: Forgive me . . . Forgive me . . . Ladies and Gentlemen.

[*He throws down kisses as fast as he can and flies right away.*]

FIRST POLICEMAN [*to the vanishing Amédée*]: You might at least drop the other shoe!

MADELEINE [*wringing her hands*]: Amédée, Amédée, your career in the theatre!

MADO [*to the Soldier*]: He must be a writer!

SOLDIER: Gee! A writer . . . that's swell! . . .

MAN [*to Madeleine*]: Why don't you let him alone!

MADELEINE [*to the vanished Amédée*]: You've forgotten your mackintosh, you'll only make yourself ill! Amédée!

[*Amédée's second shoe falls from on high.*]

SECOND POLICEMAN: Well, that's very thoughtful!

FIRST POLICEMAN: That makes us one each!

[*The* POLICEMEN *take a shoe each.*]

WOMAN: And what about us?

[*A jacket and some cigarettes fall from above.*]

MAN: Cigarettes! A jacket!

[*They all share them out.*]

MADO: He's not what you'd call stingy!

[*The sky is full of brilliant lights: comets, shooting stars, etc.*] Ooh! Fireworks!

MAN: Rockets!

WOMAN: Not real ones!

MADELEINE [*to the sky*]: Come along now, Amédée, won't you ever be serious?

SECOND POLICEMAN [*looking up at the sky and wagging his finger at Amédée as one would at a child*]: You little rascal, you! Little rascal!

ALL [*imitating the Policeman's gesture*]: Little rascal! Little rascal!

SOLDIER: Why, Junior, you bad boy!
  [*Brilliant flashes. Blazing lights from all sides.*]

WOMAN: He's out of sight. He's vanished!

MADELEINE [*to the sky*]: Amédée, you haven't even finished your play!

MADO [*to Madeleine*]: I shouldn't worry about him!

WOMAN: Men are all alike!

MADO [*to Madeleine*]: He might come back to you!

WOMAN: Oh no! He won't come back!
  [MADELEINE *turns her head from one to the other.*]

MAN [*to Woman*]: Why do you say that? What do you know about it?

MADO: Oh yes, he might!

WOMAN: Of course he won't! Exactly the same thing happened to me with my first husband! I never saw him again!

MADELEINE [*to herself*]: Amédée, you may have gone up in the world, but you're not going up in *my* estimation!
  [*The dead man's big hat falls from above, with the beard too, if possible, and lands on Madeleine's head. She drops to the ground and sits there, the hat on her head and the beard round her neck.*]

MAN: Perhaps he was a genius!

SECOND POLICEMAN: All that talent wasted! It's a bad day for literature!

MADO: No one's indispensable!

SOLDIER: She's crying!

MADO: He's left her the flat, anyway!

SECOND POLICEMAN: Let me help you up! [*Assisting her*] Let me buy you a drink!

MADELEINE [*rising painfully to her feet, supported by the* POLICE-MAN, *she goes on sobbing and repeating till the end of the play*]: No, no. I'm not thirsty, I'm not thirsty!

MADO [*to the Soldier*]: You take me to America with you?

SOLDIER: To the United States of America? . . .

MAN [*to Woman*]: Come on, Julie. Let's go to bed!

WOMAN [*to Man*]: We'll close the shutters, the show's over!

FIRST POLICEMAN [*in the orchestra pit, whistle in hand, turning towards the audience*]: Move along there, please, Ladies and Gentlemen, hurry along there, move along, please . . .

CURTAIN

ARTHUR ADAMOV

PROFESSOR TARANNE

Translated by Peter Meyer

No performance or public reading of this play
may take place without application before
rehearsals commence to Margaret Ramsay
Ltd, 14 Goodwin's Court, London WC 2,
acting in conjunction with Odette Arnaud, 11
rue de Téhéran, Paris

PROFESSOR TARANNE

First performed by the Roger Planchon company at Lyons, 1953

CHARACTERS

PROFESSOR TARANNE
THE CHIEF INSPECTOR
THE JUNIOR CLERK (a man)
THE OLD CLERK (a woman)
A WOMAN JOURNALIST
FIRST GENTLEMAN
SECOND GENTLEMAN
A SMART WOMAN
THIRD GENTLEMAN
FOURTH GENTLEMAN
THE HOTEL MANAGERESS
FIRST POLICEMAN
SECOND POLICEMAN
JEANNE

SCENE ONE

———◆———

A Police station

> [*In the left fore ground, seated behind a desk covered with papers, the* CHIEF INSPECTOR, *an elderly man, strongly built. He is wearing a black coat and striped trousers. Standing very stiffly in front of the desk,* PROFESSOR TARANNE. *About forty years old. He too is dressed in black. On their right, a little to the rear, sitting astride a chair, with his chin resting on the back, a very dark young man, the* JUNIOR CLERK.*
>
> *In the left background, a woman, the* OLD CLERK, *wearing a printed summer dress, checks papers, opens drawers, examines cards.*
>
> *On the right the stage is empty.*]

TARANNE [*gasping a little, in a single outburst*]: But anyway you know my name! I'm famous, I'm respected. You should know that like everyone else; in your profession, I'd even say better than everyone else. You know quite well this accusation's false. Why should I do it? The way I've always lived is proof I couldn't descend to such behaviour .... And after all, a little common sense, please! Who on earth would take all his clothes off in this cold weather? [*Laughing*] I've no desire to be ill and go to bed for weeks; like all hard-working men, I'm a miser with my time....

So do think! Can you trust the evidence of children? They say ... whatever comes into their head. To make themselves interesting, to make people notice them, they'll do anything. ... You must know children. And I do know them. Not that I teach them, [*Importantly*] I'm a university professor. ... But ... [*Turning towards the Old Clerk who is still sorting her papers*] ... my sister has a little girl. A little girl who wants, at any price, to be taken seriously. You must listen to her. Listen to her! Besides I like her very much. I can say I like all children. But to go as far as believing what they say....

I was walking quietly at the edge of the lake and then suddenly I saw them. They were there, quite close, they surrounded me . . . And others appeared, from everywhere at the same time. They all came at me. Then I began to run. I don't know why I ran . . . probably because I didn't expect to see them there.

Certainly I ran. They could have told you I ran, but that's all. Look at me: do I look like a man who's got dressed in a hurry? And when would I have the time to get dressed . . .?

INSPECTOR: I'm sorry. But I've a report here that doesn't agree at all with what you say.

TARANNE: They were running, and shouting all together. [*Quietly*] As if they'd been given the cue.

INSPECTOR: What were they shouting?

TARANNE [*in a shrill, little voice, and pointing his finger*]: 'You'll see! You'll see!' But see what? I've done nothing wrong, and I can prove it.

INSPECTOR: We only want to find out the truth.

TARANNE: I am Professor Taranne, I'm famous. I have given a great many lectures abroad. Only recently I was invited to Belgium, and achieved an unheard-of-success . . . All the young people flocked to my discussions . . . they fought to get a single sheet of paper in my handwriting . . .

INSPECTOR [*rising and putting his hand on Professor Taranne's shoulder*]: I have no doubt about your success. But for the moment that is not what matters. [*He removes his hand. Pause.*] We must clear up this affair to complete the report. [*He remains standing.*]

TARANNE: Report? What report? But if you make a report, you may cause me serious harm . . . compromise my career.

INSPECTOR [*sitting down again*]: You're not the first man such things have happened to. [*Pause.*] You'll get off with a fine, that's all. If you can pay it, this incident won't have any consequences for you.

TARANNE: Of course I can pay. I have money. I'll sign you

a cheque, nothing easier. [*Putting his hand in his pocket*] Right away if you like . . .

INSPECTOR [*rising again and touching Professor Taranne's arm*]: No, not right away. I'm only asking you to sign [*pointing to a sheet of paper on the desk*] a statement admitting that you were surprised naked by children just before dark. [*He sits down again.*] You can add that you didn't know you were being watched.

TARANNE: I know only too well I'm being watched, peered at, everybody has his eyes fixed on me.

Why do they look at me like this? I don't look at anyone. Usually I lower my eyes. Sometimes even I almost close them. [*Pause.*] I had my eyes almost closed when they appeared, all of them.

INSPECTOR: How many were there?

TARANNE: I didn't count them, I didn't have time. [*Pause.*] Why do you ask me that? I've told you who I am. That should be enough for you . . . I can't believe you've never heard of me.

INSPECTOR [*laughing*]: I'm sorry.

TARANNE: And so you should be. You ought to know who you're dealing with. [*Vehemently*] Once again, how can you trust the prattle of children? What proof is there that the girl, who came here to tell you all this, was really present . . . at the scene? Other children must have told it her the way they do and she changed it again, transformed it, perhaps without even realizing. [*Pause.*] Yes, of course that's what happened.

Besides, it's quite simple, you've only to send for people who know me. I can give you their names and credentials. They'll bear witness to my character . . . and my reputation. [*Pause.*] Make them come here, all of them! Anyone you like, anyone! And you'll see . . .

[*A JOURNALIST enters right, a fair woman, middle-aged, neither ugly nor pretty, her hair cut in an Eton crop. She is wearing a pleated skirt and short-sleeved blouse.*]

JOURNALIST: You haven't seen a gentleman who's very tall

and well-built? He always holds his glasses in his hand. He
arranged to meet me here . . .

JUNIOR CLERK: No, Madam, no one's been here, except
[*pointing to Professor Taranne*] the Professor.

[PROFESSOR TARANNE *gives a start.*]

TARANNE [*approaching the Journalist*]: I think we've already
met . . . If I remember correctly, you have recently published a thesis . . . [*turning towards the Junior Clerk*] . . . a
thesis which is quite remarkable.

JOURNALIST [*unembarrassed, as she's walking*]: You must have
made a mistake. I'm a journalist. [*To the Junior Clerk*]
How hot it is in here! You couldn't let a little air in?

JUNIOR CLERK: With pleasure.

[*He rises, but the* OLD CLERK *has anticipated him and goes
through the action of opening the window at the back. He sits
down again and takes up his old position, his chin resting on
the back of his chair.*]

TARANNE [*to the Journalist*]: Allow me to introduce myself . . .

JOURNALIST [*turning her back on him and going towards the
Chief Inspector who is still writing*]: Really, men have no
imagination. When they want to accost a woman, they've
always met her somewhere.

[*The* INSPECTOR *laughs gently as he goes on writing. The*
JOURNALIST *goes to the window at the back.*

The FIRST *and* SECOND GENTLEMEN *enter right in winter
overcoats, very busy. The* FIRST GENTLEMAN *carries a
leather briefcase. They are obviously continuing a conversation
which has already begun.*

FIRST GENTLEMAN [*to the Second*]: I did tell you not to trust
him.

TARANNE [*hesitates and then approaches the Two Gentlemen*]:
I'm so glad to meet you. You can do me . . . a service.

[*The two men look at each other, taken aback; they think
Professor Taranne is mad.*]

FIRST GENTLEMAN [*coldly*]: I don't know you, sir.

[*The* SECOND GENTLEMAN *makes a gesture with his hand,
meaning: 'Neither do I.'*]

TARANNE: What? But I've seen you so often at my lectures . . .

SECOND GENTLEMAN: We don't go to any lectures. [*Laughing*] We've passed the age for examinations. [*To the First Gentleman, importantly*] He must be forced to change his progamme.

> [*The* FIRST GENTLEMAN *takes the arm of the Second. They walk up and down like sentries.*]

TARANNE [*following them*]: But, gentlemen, you can't not recognize me, it's impossible. I am . . . Professor Taranne.

FIRST GENTLEMAN [*slowly as if trying to remember*]: Taranne?

SECOND GENTLEMAN [*pointedly turning his back on Taranne and taking the First Gentleman by the arm*]: In any case you can rely on my cooperation.

TARANNE [*stammering*]: Please, gentlemen, do make an effort, just a tiny effort. And perhaps . . . in less than a minute, you'll cry out – [*happily*] Why, it's Taranne!

SECOND GENTLEMAN [*shrugging his shoulders*]: You can see we're busy.

> [THE PROFESSOR *stands bewildered.*]

FIRST GENTLEMAN [*to the Second, taking him by the arm*]: It's time to take action.

> [*They take a few steps.*]

TARANNE [*going towards the Chief Inspector, who is still sitting at his desk*]: I can't understand it. Because after all, quite apart from my honours . . . my work . . . I've a face you don't forget once you've seen it.

INSPECTOR: Of course.

TARANNE: It's true that in the meantime I've made a long trip abroad.

INSPECTOR: I know. A trip which was a very great success.

TARANNE: An extraordinary success. And I must go there again very soon. [*Pause.*] Abroad, the problems that interest me are examined much more seriously. They are given an importance they don't always have here, that I must say.

[*The* CHIEF INSPECTOR *does not move.* PROFESSOR TARANNE *timidly approaches the Two Gentlemen again. The* JUNIOR CLERK, *who has remained in the same position, seems to have fallen asleep. The* OLD CLERK *is still checking papers.*]

JOURNALIST [*leaving the window and going to meet the Two Gentlemen*]: But I didn't recognize you. Really, I do apologize.

SECOND GENTLEMAN: The way one meets people!

TARANNE: I've often noticed . . .

SECOND GENTLEMAN [*to the First Gentleman, once again turning his back on Professor Taranne*]: I consider it important to act quickly.

[*They walk up and down.*]

JOURNALIST: It's the matter you spoke to me about the other day?

FIRST GENTLEMAN [*laughing*]: We can't hide anything from you.

[*A* SMART WOMAN *enters, elderly, wearing dark clothes and a hat with a small veil, accompanied by the* THIRD *and* FOURTH GENTLEMEN, *both tall and well dressed, their hair greying at the temples.*]

SECOND GENTLEMAN: What a surprise!

[*General hand-shaking.*]

JOURNALIST [*playfully, to the Third Gentleman*]: How small the world is!

THIRD GENTLEMAN [*turning towards the Smart Woman and the Fourth Gentleman, in a low voice*]: She's a journalist and works so hard. You meet her everywhere, even in University precincts!

[*General hand-shaking.* PROFESSOR TARANNE *gives a start and approaches.*]

FOURTH GENTLEMAN: I read your last article. Congratulations!

SMART WOMAN [*seriously*]: Talking of universities . . . last week I attended a lecture which particularly interested me. [*Suddenly noticing Professor Taranne*] But I'm not dreaming, it's . . . [*To Professor Taranne*] Professor, I never dared hope for such luck. I was just talking about you.

TARANNE [*stuttering with emotion*]: I'm delighted . . .

SMART WOMAN: Professor, allow me to introduce you to my friends. [*Pointing to Professor Taranne*] Professor Ménard.

TARANNE [*crushed*]: I . . .

> [*The* CHIEF INSPECTOR *arranges the papers on his desk, rises, puts on his overcoat, and goes out left. No one seems to see him go.*]

FOURTH GENTLEMAN [*almost shouting, leaning towards the Smart Woman*]: Come now! That isn't Professor Ménard. He's rather like him, but Professor Ménard is much taller, well-built . . .

THIRD GENTLEMAN: He holds his glasses in his hand . . . like he does. [*Laughing*] But apart from that!

TARANNE [*stammering*]: I . . . am Professor Taranne . . . You must . . . of course know my work.

SMART WOMAN. Taranne?

> [*The* THIRD *and* FOURTH GENTLEMEN *make a movement of the hand, meaning 'We don't know him either.'*
> *The* JUNIOR CLERK *rises, puts his chair near the desk, and goes out left. No one seems to see him go.*]

TARANNE [*stuttering*]: You amaze me . . . Expecially because I know Professor Ménard . . . and particularly admire him and . . . for his part . . . he has the greatest [*his voice fills with despair*] respect for me.

> [*Professor Taranne has spoken to the empty air; no one was listening. The* SMART WOMAN *takes the arm of the Third and Fourth Gentlemen. Slowly they take a few steps.*
> *The* OLD CLERK, *who has finished her work, puts on her overcoat and goes out left, once again without anyone seeming to notice.*]

JOURNALIST [*in the wings*]: I must be going now.

> [*She waves her hand in farewell and goes out right.*]

SECOND GENTLEMAN [*putting his hand on the First Gentleman's shoulder*]: This imposture must cease now. Immediately! We'll put things right.

SMART WOMAN [*to the Fourth Gentleman*]: Shall we go? We're not going to stay here for ever [*suddenly very serious*] like criminals . . .

[*The* SMART WOMAN *and the* THIRD *and* FOURTH GENTLEMEN *go out right.* PROFESSOR TARANNE *takes a step towards them, but very quickly stops and leans unsteadily on a chair; then he suddenly notices the absence of the Chief Inspector and the Clerks, and begins to run. He goes out right.*]

TARANNE [*off-stage*]: Excuse me . . . but I wanted to ask you if you'd seen the Inspector or one of the clerks . . . It's most annoying. I should have signed my statement . . . and . . . I haven't. [*Terrified*] But they can't have left, one of us would have seen them. I don't understand . . .

[*The* MANAGERESS *enters left. She moves the chairs and desk a little, takes away the files and brings in a board with keys on it, which she hangs on the wall backstage right.*

The scene now represents a Hotel Office.]

CURTAIN

SCENE TWO

——◆◆◆——

A Hotel

[PROFESSOR TARANNE *is walking up and down.*]

TARANNE: Still nobody! How infuriating! The manageress has gone for a walk . . . as usual. The way she behaves, she'd do better to give notice, it would be more honest . . . [*Pause.*] All the same I'd like to know if there are any letters for me.

[*Two Policemen enter right; commonplace appearance.*]

Who are you? What do you want? There's no one in the office.

FIRST POLICEMAN: We're looking for someone called ...
[*He pulls a document from his pocket.*]

SECOND POLICEMAN: Taranne.

TARANNE: You mean – Professor Taranne.

FIRST POLICEMAN [*pointing to a document in his hand*]: The profession's left blank.

TARANNE: That's most annoying. Because how can I be sure I'm the man you're looking for?
[*The* POLICEMEN *laugh.*]
I am Professor Taranne, I have a chair at the University ...
[*The* POLICEMEN *move towards him.*]
What's the matter? I've done no harm to anyone. [*Laughing*] My conscience is clear.

FIRST POLICEMAN: You've committed an offence against the regulations.

TARANNE: Explain what you mean ...

SECOND POLICEMAN: Nothing we'd like better, but you're interrupting us.

FIRST POLICEMAN: The offence you've committed is a very small one. You'll be let off with a warning.

TARANNE: Once again I insist on knowing what this is all about.

FIRST POLICEMAN: Stop worrying. Who's never been summonsed some time or other?

TARANNE [*after a silence, as if taking a heroic decision*]: Oh, I see. You're not up to date. But I've just come straight from the police station. I've signed the necessary papers. Witnesses have stood surety for my good behaviour. The affair is settled. Anyhow you must realize that; as I'm here, before you, at liberty; and I must explain ...
    Your department's very badly organized, I must say. Because after all, what I'm telling you now, you should know. It's the only conclusion I can draw.

SECOND POLICEMAN: You're making a mistake. We're not attached to the local station here. It's about a different crime that we've been sent to question you.

TARANNE: Once again, what do you mean . . .

FIRST POLICEMAN: You're accused of leaving paper lying about . . . in bathing cabins.

SECOND POLICEMAN: You think you can do anything you like. From now on you'll know you must leave the cabins clean.

TARANNE [*aggressively*]: You have the wrong man. It so happens I didn't . . . take a cabin, either yesterday or . . . the other day, and those are the only times I've bathed recently. [*Pause.*] Of course I usually take a cabin. I hate undressing on the beach where everyone can see me. And all the precautions you have to surround yourself with. If you don't want to be exposed to indiscreet staring, all these precautions tire me out; what's more they make me lose time I'd rather employ [*laughing*] in something . . . more useful. [*Making a vague gesture*] It's . . . such a business lowering your trousers after hurriedly tying your shirt around your belt; it might fall down, you have to be careful. [*Pause.*] You'll tell me you can always go behind the cabins, but there the sand's never changed and it's so dirty . . . I hesitate to go there.

FIRST POLICEMAN [*offering Professor Taranne the document he is holding*]: All right. We're only asking you to make the following statement: I swear I haven't occupied a bathing cabin since the . . . so and so, and add your signature. It's not difficult.

SECOND POLICEMAN: After 'since the so and so', you can add, if it's right and you'd like to, 'that's because I had no money'.

TARANNE: It's true, I had no money . . . on me. That can happen to anyone, leaving your money at home. Of course it may seem odd that the same thing should happen again a few days later. But if you really think about it, that's a most superficial view. . . . Things always happen in series. It's strange, but . . . it's a fact. Yes, last time I went to the beach, I forgot my money again. . . .

You'll tell me I could have gone back for it, retraced my

steps. But that I cannot do, I never have been able to. To go along a road with the thought of having to go along it again, see all the details afresh, I haven't the strength to. [*Changing his tone.*] Besides, generally speaking, I don't like walking. I can't work while I walk.

SECOND POLICEMAN [*taking a notebook out of his pocket*]: Do you recognize this?

TARANNE: But that's my notebook. . . . How have you got it? Answer me. I order you to answer me. I always have it on me, I'm never without it. I note in it all the ideas that come to me in the course of the day, ideas I develop later. . . . No, you won't find the full text of a single one of my lectures. [*Laughing.*] The whole notebook wouldn't be big enough. . . . My lectures are long, very long. A friend once assured me that nothing so long is delivered in any University. I'm entitled to several hours continuously. . . . Sometimes even, I'm on the rostrum till late at night. . . . While I'm speaking, the lamps are lit and through the open doors new students never cease to enter. Naturally I don't much like that, because of the noise, the chairs they move. . . . But during the day a lot of people have jobs they can't get away from, however much they want to. . . . You must put yourself in their place. Especially as my teaching doesn't suffer from this state of affairs. My lectures are sub-divided in such a way that you can easily follow one part without necessarily having heard what has gone before. . . . It's not that I repeat myself, no. But at the beginning of each . . . part, I summarize what I've said before, and this summary, far from being useless, sheds new light on the question I'm dealing with.

FIRST POLICEMAN: In your notebook there are several pages in a handwriting which isn't yours.

SECOND POLICEMAN [*holding out the notebook to Professor Taranne without giving it to him*]: Here for instance.

[*The two* POLICEMEN *close in on Professor Taranne.*]

TARANNE [*leaning over his notebook, which the second Policeman is still holding*]: But no, look, it is me, it is. I recognize it plainly. My writing's so individual!

SECOND POLICEMAN: Then read us what you've written.

TARANNE [*trying to decipher the page he is shown*]: I want ... would ... wish.... It's a fact, I find it difficult to decipher. But that doesn't prove anything. When you write very quickly, as you walk, for example, and I often write as I walk, it does happen that you can't read it.

FIRST POLICEMAN: The author of a notebook ought to be able to complete what he finds hard to read ... in his own notebook.

SECOND POLICEMAN: It looks as though....

TARANNE [*terrified*]: I wanted to steal someone else's writing? But why? For what reason?

FIRST POLICEMAN [*laughing*]: I don't know. To change some of. ...

TARANNE [*stretching out his hand*]: Please, give it back to me. [*The* SECOND POLICEMAN *hides the notebook behind his back.*]

FIRST POLICEMAN: Not so fast!

SECOND POLICEMAN: One more question. Why are the pages at each end of the book the only ones written on? The pages in the middle are. ...

TARANNE: The pages in the middle? No, I don't believe it. A long time ago, I completely filled this notebook. It's ... a very old book I took to read again, to look for some facts I needed. I remember ... I wrote on every page, even in the margins. You must have noticed. It's all been filled by me, by me, do you hear?

SECOND POLICEMAN [*giving him the notebook*]: See for yourself.

FIRST POLICEMAN: You haven't used all the pages yet, that's all.

TARANNE: Yes, it's true ... there's a gap. A gap in the middle!

SECOND POLICEMAN [*laughing*]: That's what we told you.

TARANNE: I'll explain.... It's very simple.... Sometimes I

open my notebooks at one end, sometimes at the other. . . .
You understand. . . . Oh, I can see your objections. You're
going to say 'But then why is it always written in the same
direction? If you'd started at both ends, we wouldn't be
able to read it straight through.' Of course. . . . Only I pay
attention. . . .

[*The two* POLICEMEN *go out right. Taranne does not notice
them go and continues to speak.*]

Obviously I could have taken care not to jump pages, and
. . . this wouldn't have happened. . . . But you see I'm
absentminded. . . . Many scholars, seekers after know-
ledge, are. . . . Why, nearly all of them are, it's well-known.
[*Laughing*] There are stories about it. [*Suddenly noticing he's
alone, he goes out quickly right. Off-stage*] Wait . . . I haven't
signed my statement. You haven't even given me a pen,
and I haven't one on me. . . . Upstairs, I left it upstairs! But
I couldn't go and get it. . . . I don't know why, my key isn't
on the board, and the Manageress gone out as usual! Do
you hear me? . . . [*Shouting*] Hullo! [*After a moment, he enters
again right, the notebook still in his hand. Walking*] I don't
understand why they've left like this, without saying anything. They come, and go . . . they think it's quite natural
to disturb a man who's working, and needs a little quiet to
put his work in order.

[*He takes a few steps. The* MANAGERESS *enters left, carrying under her arm an immense roll of paper. Going towards
her*:]

Are there any letters for me?

MANAGERESS: No, Professor, only this. I was asked to give it
to you immediately. [*She holds out the roll of paper.*]

TARANNE [*taking it*]: Thank you.

[*The Manageress goes out. Professor Taranne places the notebook on the desk, kneels down, and unrolls the paper in the middle
of the stage. It is a gigantic map with a plan, drawn in Indian
ink. Professor Taranne on his knees leans over the map. Stammering*:]

There must be a mistake. This certainly can't be addressed

to me. . . . Yet, Professor Taranne, it really is for me, there's no doubt about it. [*Shouting*] Madam!

[*The* MANAGERESS *enters left.*]

MANAGERESS: You called me, Professor?

TARANNE [*rising*]: Who brought you this map?

MANAGERESS: I found it on the desk, when I came in. There was a piece of paper attached and on it was written: 'To be given to Professor Taranne immediately'. That's all I know.

[*The* MANAGERESS *goes out left.*

PROFESSOR TARANNE *kneels again in front of the map and studies it.* JEANNE *enters right, a dark young woman with regular features and an even voice. She shows no surprise and goes round the map to avoid walking on it. She stops on the other side of the map on the left of the stage.*]

JEANNE: It's nice here.

TARANNE: Jeanne, the most extraordinary things are happening to me.

JEANNE: Extraordinary! Are you sure? According to you, everything's always extraordinary. [*Laughing*] What a brother I have!

TARANNE: Listen to me carefully. . . . I've just been brought . . . this map. . . . It's the plan of the dining-room on a ship where I seem to have booked a passage. Only you see, I haven't booked a passage on a ship. . . .

JEANNE [*kneels and leans over the map*]: To judge from this plan, it's a large, beautiful dining-room.

TARANNE: Yes, it is large.

JEANNE: I've often admired photographs of the *President Welling* in travel agencies. It's certainly the fastest, most luxurious liner there is.

TARANNE: That may be. The fact remains that I haven't booked a passage on this ship, or any other, and so. . . .

JEANNE [*leaning farther over, her hand flat on the map*]: What are you complaining about? You've been highly honoured. [*Pointing to a place on the map*] You see, the cross there, that's your place. You're at the Captain's table, and in the centre too.

TARANNE: None of that explains why I should have booked a passage on a liner. To go where? You don't go to Belgium by liner, as far as I know.

JEANNE: To have given you such a good place, they must know who you are.

TARANNE: Of course. . . . It's not by chance they've put me at the Captain's table, next to the most important people. . . . But I have no intention of going so far away. I have no reason to. I've nothing to go for . . . or to fear.

JEANNE [*rises and holds herself very upright*]: You must have taken your ticket one day when you were tired through working too hard. And now you're not so tired and you've forgotten you took it.

TARANNE [*absently*]: Perhaps.

JEANNE: Yes, it does happen that people do things they forget later. Often I can't find my combs and I have them in my hair. It's funny, you're a little annoyed for the moment and then you laugh. . . . [*She laughs; then seriously*] I have a letter for you.

TARANNE [*very quickly*]: From Belgium?

JEANNE: I don't know. There's a statue on the stamp, and some writing.

TARANNE: You have the letter? [*He goes towards Jeanne, walking round the map.*]

JEANNE [*taking the letter out of her pocket*]: Above the statue is written [*Reading*] Territory of Independence.

TARANNE: There's no such writing on any stamp! [*Stretching out his hand*] Give it to me.

JEANNE [*showing him the letter without giving it to him*]: You see, next to it there's another stamp with a lion.

TARANNE: Yes, the royal lion of Belgium!

JEANNE: I had to pay a surcharge. [*Laughing*] I've completely emptied my purse.

TARANNE: It's just as I thought. The Rector's letter at last. [*Pause.*] Give it to me. Why won't you give it to me?

JEANNE: I wanted to read it to you.

TARANNE: Give it to me.

[*He wants to take the letter, but* JEANNE *resists.*]

JEANNE [*offering him the letter*]: As you wish!

TARANNE: No, read it.

[JEANNE *sits on the edge of the desk and opens the envelope.* PROFESSOR TARANNE *remains standing, next to her.*]

JEANNE [*reading in a neutral voice which she retains until the end of the play*]: 'Sir, your last letter showed evidence of impatience which, I must confess, surprised me. . . .'

TARANNE [*frightened*]: I knew it. I've been clumsy, I've annoyed him. . . .

JEANNE [*reading*]: 'However, I thought that by drawing your attention to my wife's state of health, I had sufficiently explained the reason for my delay in answering you. . . .'

TARANNE: Of course, I should have asked him for news of his wife. But he might have put himself in my place. In my letter I spoke of questions I have particularly at heart. It's not so easy to pass from one subject to another. [*Pause.*] Oh well, yes, I did forget his wife.

JEANNE [*reading*]: 'Under these conditions I cannot possibly make the arrangements which your second visit would require. . . .'

TARANNE: So he thinks he's irreplaceable. . . . There are other people just as capable of making the arrangements as he is. . . . Other people would be happy to do me a service, take all the necessary steps.

JEANNE [*reading*]: 'I must also tell you I was surprised to learn that on your last visit you had neglected to inform the Secretariat of the exact hours of your lectures, thereby inconveniencing your colleagues, who had to change their timetables at the last moment. . . .'

TARANNE: But they were delighted!

JEANE [*reading*]: 'I have also learnt that your discussions were prolonged beyond the time permitted. . . .'

TARANNE: I only prolonged my lectures because the wealth of subject matter forced me to . . . I couldn't do anything else. . . .

JEANNE [*reading*]: 'Finally I've been told that your students' attention abated considerably; some of them went so far as to talk out loud and left the hall before you had finished.'

TARANNE: Who has dared to tell him such lies? And how can he be as credulous as this?

It's absurd! If the hall had emptied while I was lecturing, I'd have seen it, I'd have stopped. . . . Now, I never stopped. . . . On the contrary I spoke continuously, and without lowering my voice. [*Pause.*] I never lowered my voice for a moment.

I know some students happened to leave before the end. But that's because they had a train to catch. They came from another town, specially to hear me, and that was the only train there was. . . . These students can't be blamed in any way, any way at all. . . .

As for the murmurs that arose once at the back of the hall, I know what provoked them . . . some girls had to silence two or three young men who were sitting behind them and shouting 'What clear thinking! What powerful reasoning!' I'm not angry with them: they were conscientiously taking notes. It's absolutely normal that they should insist on silence.

JEANNE [*reading*]: 'All this would be of little importance, if only the interest of your lectures could not be questioned, but that is not the case. Your recent expositions have seemed to me most uneven. . . .'

TARANNE: Uneven! Easy to say! As if you could always go straight to the point! As if there were no questions you have to explore more than others, because they concern you personally, touch you. . . . [*He taps his chest with his finger.*]

JEANNE [*reading*]: 'Certain points did interest me. But I should have liked to see them developed with more precision, and, I may say, with more honesty. The ideas you express remind me rather too much of Professor Ménard's, which are already so highly esteemed. Not that I make the slightest reservation about these ideas. On the contrary, I think they deserve the greatest attention. But how could you neglect to indicate your references, and so present, as the result of your personal research, the reproduction of a work which we all know and admire. . . .'

TARANNE [*leaning defeated on the table, and stammering*]. It's not true. . . . It's not true. . . . We had the same ideas at the same moment. These things happen. It's not the first time.

JEANNE [*reading*] : 'I should not perhaps have informed you of my impressions, if I had not received letters from various sources, pointing out what I must really call your lack of delicacy.'

TARANNE [*standing up straight, with a start*] : They've written to him, all of them! I knew they would. I watched them carefully. While I was speaking, they were yapping. [*Shouting in a shrill voice*] 'He's stolen Professor Ménard's spectacles. He does everything like Professor Ménard. Pity he's smaller than he is.' And I don't know what nonsense. . . .

If only they'd had the courage to get up and say to my face the things they whisper so cravenly, then I should have risen and I should have said : [*With an orator's gesture, raising his voice*] Gentlemen. . . .

JEANNE [*reading*] : 'As a result of the facts I have mentioned, I cannot invite you to our next congress.

'Believe me, I am sorry to have to change the opinion I had formed of you.'

[JEANNE *rises, puts the letter quietly on the desk, and gets ready to go out.* PROFESSOR TARANNE *clutches at the desk to avoid falling.*]

TARANNE: Why tell me this now, after all these years? Why hasn't he told me sooner? Why haven't they all told me? Because it's obvious! You can see it at once!

[*While* PROFESSOR TARANNE *is talking,* JEANNE *carefully walks round the map and goes out slowly right.*

After his last sentence, PROFESSOR TARANNE *turns towards the map and looks at it for a long time.*

The MANAGERESS *enters left. Without looking at Professor Taranne, she picks up the few objects which constitute the décor (chairs, etc.) and carries them into the wings. The stage remains bare.*

136

Only the notebook and the letter which the Manageress has dropped are lying on the ground. PROFESSOR TARANNE *has noticed nothing. When the* MANAGERESS *has gone, he takes the map, goes mechanically to the back of the stage, and looks for a place to hang it. A device is already installed. By standing on tiptoe, he succeeds in hanging the map on the wall. The map is a large expanse, grey, uniform, absolutely empty.*
Professor Taranne, his back to the audience, looks at it for a long moment, then very slowly begins to take off his clothes.]

CURTAIN

FERNANDO ARRABAL

THE TWO EXECUTIONERS

Melodrama in One Act

Translated by Barbara Wright

THE TWO EXECUTIONERS

CHARACTERS

THE TWO EXECUTIONERS, I don't know their names
The Mother, FRANÇOISE
The Two Sons, BENOÎT and MAURICE
The Husband, JEAN

*The action takes place in a very dark room. Left, a door opening on to
the road. At the back, the door which gives on to the torture chamber.
Bare walls. In the middle of the room, a table and three chairs.*

[*It is dark. The Two* EXECUTIONERS *are alone, sitting on
the chairs. There is an insistent knock at the street door. It really
looks as if the executioners can't hear anything. The door opens
slowly, not without creaking. A woman's head appears. The
woman inspects the room. She decides to come in and goes up to
the executioners.*]

FRANÇOISE: Good morning, gentlemen. . . . Excuse me. . . .
Am I disturbing you?

[*The* EXECUTIONERS *remain motionless, as if it was nothing
to do with them.*]

If I'm disturbing you I'll go away. . . . [*Silence. It looks as if
the woman is trying to pluck up courage. Finally she brings herself to
speak and the words come tumbling out.*] I came to see you because I can't stand it any longer. It's about my husband.
[*Pathetically*] The being in whom I placed all my hopes, the
man to whom I gave the best years of my life and whom I
loved as I would never have thought I could love. [*Speaking
more softly, calmer*] Yes, yes, yes, he is guilty.

[*Suddenly the* EXECUTIONERS *take an interest in what the
woman is saying. One of them takes out a pencil and notebook.*]
Yes, he's guilty. He lives at number eight rue du Travail,
and his name is Jean Lagune.

[*The* EXECUTIONER *makes a note of it. As soon as he has
done so the* EXECUTIONERS *go out by the street door. A car is
heard driving off.* FRANÇOISE *also goes out by the street
door.*]

VOICE OF FRANÇOISE: Come in, children, come in.

VOICE OF BENOÎT: There's not much light here.

VOICE OF FRANÇOISE: Yes, the room is very dark. It
frightens me, but we must go in. We've got to wait for
Daddy.

[*Enter* FRANÇOISE *and her two sons,* BENOÎT *and* MAURICE.]

FRANÇOISE: Sit down, children. Don't be afraid.

[*All three sit down round the table.*]

FRANÇOISE [*she always speaks in a whining voice*]: What sad and dramatic moments we are living through! What sins are we guilty of, that life should punish us so cruelly?

BENOÎT: Don't worry, Mother. Don't cry.

FRANÇOISE: No, my son, I'm not crying, I shan't cry, I shall stand up to all the dangers that beset us. How I love to see you always so solicitous about everything that concerns me! But just look at your brother Maurice – as unnatural as ever.

[MAURICE, *with a melancholy air, looks apparently deliberately in the opposite direction from his mother.*]

Look at him; today, when more than ever I need your support, he turns against me and overwhelms me with scorn. What harm have I ever done you, unworthy son? Speak to me, say something.

BENOÎT: Don't take any notice of him, Mother, he doesn't know anything about the gratitude one owes to a mother.

FRANÇOISE [*to Maurice*]: Can't you hear your brother? Listen to him. If anyone said such a thing to me I'd die of shame. But *you* aren't ashamed. Good God! What a cross!

BENOÎT: Gently, Mother, don't let him upset you. He'll never agree with you.

FRANÇOISE: Yes, my son, you don't realize. When it isn't your father, it's Maurice: nothing but suffering. And when I've always been their slave. Just look what a gay life so many women of my age lead, enjoying themselves night and day going to dances, cafés, cinemas! So many women! You can't realize it properly you're still too young. I could have done the same, but I preferred to sacrifice myself for my husband and for you, silently, humbly, without expecting anything from my sacrifices, and even knowing that one day the beings who have been the dearest to me would say what your brother says today – that I haven't done enough. Can you see, my son, how they reward my sacrifices? You can see – by always returning evil for good, always.

BENOÎT: How good you are! How good you are!

FRANÇOISE: But what good does it do me to know that? It comes to the same thing. Everything comes to the same thing. I don't feel like doing anything any more, I don't care about anything, nothing is important to me any more. I just want to be good and always sacrifice myself for you, without expecting anything for my sacrifices, and even knowing that one day the beings who have been the dearest to me, those who ought to be grateful for all my concern for them, deliberately ignore my sacrifices. All my life I've been a martyr to you, and I shall continue to be a martyr until God chooses to recall me to Him.

BENOÎT: Dearest Mother!

FRANÇOISE: Yes, my son, I live only for you. How can I have any other interests? Luxury, dresses, parties, the theatre – none of these count for me, I have but one care: you. What does the rest matter?

BENOÎT [to Maurice]: Maurice, do you hear what Mother says?

FRANÇOISE: Let him be, my child. Do you think I can hope that he will be able to recognize my sacrifices? No. I expect nothing from him. I even know that he probably thinks that I haven't done enough.

BENOÎT [to Maurice]: You're a good-for-nothing.

FRANÇOISE [excited]: Don't make things worse for me, Benoît, don't pick a quarrel with him. I want us to live in peace, in harmony. Whatever happens I don't want you brothers to quarrel.

BENOÎT: How good you are, Mother! . . . and good to him when he's so worthless. If it weren't for the fact that you ask me to spare him, I don't know what I'd do to him. [To Maurice, aggressively] You can say thank you to Mother, Maurice, because you deserve a good thrashing.

FRANÇOISE: No, my child, no, don't hit him. I don't want

you to hit him even if he does thoroughly deserve it. I want peace and love to reign in our midst. That's the only thing I ask of you, Benoît.

BENOÎT: Don't worry, I'll do what you ask.

FRANÇOISE: Thank you, my son. You are like balm for the injuries that life has inflicted upon me. You see, God in his infinite goodness has finally granted me a son like you to bind up the wounds my poor heart suffers, the grief caused me, to my great distress, by the beings I have struggled for the most: my husband and Maurice.

BENOÎT [angrily]: From now on, no one shall make you suffer any more.

FRANÇOISE: Don't be angry, my son, don't be upset. They've behaved badly, and they know it. What we must do is forgive them, and bear them no malice. And anyway, even though your father has sinned, sinned greatly even, you must nonetheless respect him.

BENOÎT: Respect him: *him*?

FRANÇOISE: Yes, my son. You must disregard all the sufferings he has caused. It is I who should refuse him my forgiveness, and you see, my son, I forgive him, although he has made me suffer more than I have suffered before, if that is possible, I shall continue to wait for him with open arms and I shall be able to forgive him his innumerable faults. Ever since the day I was born, life has taught me how to suffer. But I carry this cross with dignity, out of love for you.

BENOÎT: Mother, you're so good!

FRANÇOISE [in an even more humble tone]: I try, Benoît, to be good.

BENOÎT [interrupting his mother with a gesture of spontaneous affection]: Mother, you are the best woman in the world.

FRANÇOISE [humble and ashamed]: No, my son, I am not the best woman in the world, I cannot aspire to such a claim, I am too unworthy. And then, I have probably committed some sins. In spite of a great deal of good will; but even so, what counts is that I have committed some sins.

BENOÎT [*with conviction*]: No, Mother; never.

FRANÇOISE: Yes, my child, sometimes. But I can say with joy that I have always repented of them – always.

BENOÎT: You are a saint.

FRANÇOISE: Hush! What more beautiful dream could I have than saintliness! I can't be a saint. To be a saint one must be a very great person, but I am worth nothing. I simply try to be good – that is the limit of my pretensions.

[*The street door opens. Enter the two* EXECUTIONERS, *carrying Jean, Françoise's husband, who has his feet and wrists tied together and is hanging from a big stick, rather after the fashion in which captured lions or tigers are carried in Africa. Jean is gagged; as he is brought into the room he raises his head and looks at his wife, Françoise, opening his eyes very widely and perhaps with some anger.* FRANÇOISE *looks at her husband attentively, avidly even.* MAURICE *watches the procession go by with violent indignation. The two* EXECUTIONERS, *without stopping, cross the room and carry Jean from the street door into the torture chamber. All three disappear.*]

MAURICE [*to his mother, very indignantly*]: What's going on? What's the latest dirty trick?

BENOÎT [*to Maurice*]: Don't talk to Mother like that.

FRANÇOISE: Let him be, my child, let him insult me. Let him reproach me. Let him treat his mother like an enemy. Let him be, my child, let him be, God will punish this wicked action.

MAURICE: Oh, that's *too* much. [*Angrily, to his mother*] It was you who denounced him.

BENOÎT [*ready to throw himself on his brother*]: I've already told you to speak civilly to Mother. D'you understand? Civilly! D'you hear me?

FRANÇOISE: Gently, my son, gently, let him be rude to me. You know very well that he's only happy when he's making me suffer; give him that satisfaction. That's my job – to sacrifice myself for him and for you; to give you everything you want.

BENOÎT: I won't let him shout at you.

FRANÇOISE: Obey me, my son, obey me.

BENOÎT: I won't obey you. You're too good and he takes advantage of it.

[MAURICE *looks dejected.*]

FRANÇOISE: My child, do you too want to make me suffer? If he is unpleasant to me, let him be unpleasant, it was only to be expected, but you, my son, you are different – at least that's what I've always thought. Let him torture me if it does his evil heart any good.

BENOÎT: No, never; not when I'm there, at any rate.

[*The sounds of a whip can be heard, followed by cries muffled by the gag. It is Jean. The executioners are, no doubt, flogging him in the torture chamber.* FRANÇOISE *and* MAURICE *get up and go over to the torture chamber door. The mother listens avidly, her eyes wide open, a grimace on her face (almost a smile?), hysterical. The sounds of the whip become louder for a long moment. Jean groans loudly. At last the sounds of the whip and the cries cease.*]

MAURICE [*furiously, and on the verge of tears, to his mother*]: It's your fault that they're whipping Daddy. It was you who denounced him.

BENOÎT: Shut up! [*Violently*] Don't take any notice, Mother.

FRANÇOISE: Let him be, let him be, Benoît. Let him insult me. I know very well that if you weren't there he would hit me. But he's a coward and he's afraid of you, that's the only thing that stops him, because he is quite capable of lifting his hand against his mother, I can read it in his eyes. He's always been trying to.

[*A piercing moan from* JEAN. *Silence.* FRANÇOISE *makes a grimace which is almost a smile. Silence.*]

Let's go and see poor little Daddy. Let's go and see him suffering, the poor man. Because there's no doubt about it, they must have hurt him a lot. [*Grimaces from* FRANÇOISE. *Silence.* FRANÇOISE *approaches the torture chamber, half-opens the door, and, standing by the door, looks into the room. Talking to her husband, who is in the room and so can't see her*] They must have hurt you a lot, Jean. Poor Jean! You must have suffered so much, and they're going to make you suffer even more. My poor Jean!

[JEAN, *though impeded by the gag, cries out in anger.*]

Don't get into a state. It'd be better to try to be patient. You must realize that you're only at the beginning of your sufferings. You can't do anything at the moment, you're tied up, and your back's covered with blood. You can't do anything. Just calm down! And anyway, all this is going to do you a lot of good, it'll teach you to have some will power – you never did have any. [FRANÇOISE *decides to go into the room; she does so, i.e. she goes off-stage.*]

VOICE OF FRANÇOISE [*speaking as if she were at church, but out loud*]: It was I who denounced you, Jean. It was I who said you were guilty.

[JEAN *tries to speak, but as he is hindered by his gag he can only manage to make noises.* FRANÇOISE's *abnormal laugh can be heard.* MAURICE *is very worked up.* FRANÇOISE *reappears.*]

FRANÇOISE [*to her sons*]: The poor man is suffering a lot, he hasn't any patience, he never did have any.

[*Cry from* JEAN.]

MAURICE: Leave Daddy alone. Don't go on. Can't you see you're tormenting him?

FRANÇOISE: It's he who's tormenting himself; only he, and for no reason. [*She again addresses her husband through the door.*] I can see very well that it's you who are tormenting yourself. I can see very well that what I say irritates you. [*Pause – smile*] Who could pay more attention to your sufferings than I do? I shall be at your side every time you suffer. You're guilty, and it's your duty to accept your punishment with patience. You even ought to thank the executioners for taking so much trouble with you. If you were a normal, humble, just man, you'd thank the executioners, but you've always been a rebel. You needn't think you're at home now, at home where you did everything you wanted to; at the moment you're in the executioners' power. Accept your punishment without rebelling. It's your purification. Repent your sins, and promise that you won't fall back into error. And don't torment yourself with the thought that I am rejoicing to see you punished.

[*Loud groan from* JEAN.]

MAURICE: Can't you hear him groaning? Can't you see you're making him suffer? Leave him in peace!

BENOÎT: I've already told you not to talk to Mother like that.

FRANÇOISE: Let him talk to me as he wishes, my son. I'm used to it. It's my lot: to worry about them, about him and about Daddy, though they don't deserve it, and though no one thanks me for it.

[*Groans from* JEAN.]

MAURICE: Daddy! Daddy! [*On the verge of tears*] Daddy!

FRANÇOISE: He's still groaning. That's a sign that he's suffering from the wounds caused by the whip and the ropes fastening his hands and feet. [*She opens the drawer in the table and searches about inside it. Then she puts on the table a bottle of vinegar and a salt cellar which she has found in it.*] These are just what I need. I'll put vinegar and salt on his wounds to disinfect them. A bit of vinegar and salt on his wounds will do wonders! [*With hysterical enthusiasm*] A bit of salt and vinegar. Only just a tiny bit on each wound, that's all he needs.

MAURICE [*angrily*]: Don't do that.

FRANÇOISE: Is that the way you love your father? You, his favourite son, is that how you treat him? You, you of all people, wicked son! You who know very well that the executioners will flog him until death results, are you going to abandon him now and not even let me bandage his wounds? [FRANÇOISE *goes towards the torture chamber with the vinegar and salt in her hand.*]

MAURICE: Don't put salt on him! If they're going to kill him anyway, at least leave him in peace, don't make the agony worse.

FRANÇOISE: You're very young, my son, you don't know

anything about life, you haven't any experience. What would have become of you without me? Life has always been very easy for you. You're used to your mother giving you everything you want. You must remember what I say. I speak as a mother, and a mother lives only for her children. Respect your mother, respect her, if only for the white hairs which adorn her brow. Think that your mother does everything for you out of affection. When, my son, have you ever seen your mother do anything for herself? I have thought only of you. First my children, and then my husband. I don't count, not for anybody, and even less for myself. That is why, my son, now that I am going to take care of your father's wounds, you mustn't stand in my way. Others would kiss the ground I tread on. I don't ask so much from you, I merely hope that you may find it in you to thank me for my efforts. [*Pause.* FRANÇOISE *goes towards the torture chamber with the salt and vinegar.*] I'll go and put a little salt and vinegar on poor little Daddy's wounds.

[MAURICE *seizes his mother's arm brutally and prevents her from going into the room.*]

BENOÎT: Don't hold Mother's arm!

FRANÇOISE: Let him hit me. It's what he's always wanted. Look at the marks of his fingers on my poor arm. That's what he's always wanted to do – hit me.

BENOÎT [*very angry*]: How dare you hit Mother?

[BENOÎT *tries to hit his brother.* FRANÇOISE *throws herself between her sons to stop them fighting.*]

FRANÇOISE: No, my son, not in my presence. The family is sacred. I don't want my sons to fight.

[BENOÎT *controls himself with difficulty.*]

He can flay me alive if he wants to, but *please*, my child, don't hit him in my presence. I don't want any quarrels between brothers in my presence. He has hit me; but I forgive him.

[*Loud cry from her husband.*]

He is suffering – they are making him suffer .... He's suffering a great deal. I must put some vinegar on him as quickly as possible. At once. [FRANÇOISE *goes into the tor-ture chamber.*]

VOICE OF FRANÇOISE: Just a little salt and vinegar will do you a lot of good. Don't move, I haven't got much. There, there we are.

[*Groan from* JEAN.]

That's it, there, there, now a bit of salt.

[*Angry cry from Jean.*]

MAURICE [*shouts*]: Daddy! [*and weeps.*]

VOICE OF FRANÇOISE: That's it, just a tiny bit more, there, a tiny bit more, don't move. [FRANÇOISE *speaks in gasps.*] Don't move. There. Just a bit more.

[*Groan from* JEAN.]

That's it, just a bit more; there, there it'll do you good.

[*Cry from* JEAN.]

Just to finish it up, there.

[*Cry from* JEAN.]

VOICE OF FRANÇOISE: That's all I've got!

[*Long silence. Cry from* JEAN. *Silence.*]

Well now, how are your sore places? I'll touch them to see how they are.

[*Loud cry from* JEAN. MAURICE, *when his brother isn't look-ing, goes into the room.*]

VOICE OF MAURICE: What are you doing? You're scratch-ing his wounds!

[MAURICE *pushes his mother out of the room.* BENOÎT *throws himself on to his brother, about to hit him. The mother comes between them and separates the brothers.*]

FRANÇOISE: No, my son, no. [*To Benoît.*] You're hurting *me*, not him! No, don't hit your brother. I don't want you to hit him.

[BENOÎT *calms down.*]

BENOÎT: I won't tolerate him hurting you.

FRANÇOISE: Yes, let him hurt me. Let him if he enjoys it. That's what he wants. Let him. He wants me to cry when he hits me. My son, that's how your brother's made. What a martyr! What a cross! Why, O God, have I deserved to have a son who doesn't love me and who is only waiting for me to have a moment of weakness to beat and torment me!

BENOÎT [*furious*]: Maurice!

FRANÇOISE: Gently, my son, gently. [*Dejected*] What a cross! What a cross, O God! Why do you punish me thus, Lord? What have I done to provoke such a punishment? Don't fight, my children, for the sake of your poor mother who never ceases to suffer, for the sake of her white hairs. [*To Benoît*] And if *he* won't take pity on my sufferings, you at least, Benoît, must have pity on me and not make me suffer. Or can it be that you don't love me either?

  [BENOÎT, *moved, tries to say something. His mother doesn't let him speak, and continues.*]

Yes, that's it, you don't love me either.

BENOÎT [*on the verge of tears*]: Yes Mother, *I* do – *I* love you.

FRANÇOISE: Well then, why do you add extra thorns to the crown of sorrows I bear?

BENOÎT: Mother!

FRANÇOISE: Don't you see my sorrow? Don't you see the boundless sorrow of a mother?

BENOÎT [*nearly crying*]: Yes.

FRANÇOISE: Thank you, my son, you are the support of my old age. You are the unique consolation that God has given me in this life.

  [*The executioners can again be heard whipping Jean. The husband sobs. All three, FRANÇOISE and her sons, listen in silence.*]

FRANÇOISE: They're beating him again. . . . And they must be hurting him a lot. . . . [*Françoise speaks in gasps.*] He's crying! He's crying. . . . He's groaning, isn't he? [*No one answers.*] . . . Yes, yes, he's groaning, he's groaning, I can hear him perfectly. . . .

  [*Sounds of the whip, and groans.* JEAN *suddenly gives a more piercing cry. The* EXECUTIONERS *continue their blows.* JEAN *doesn't groan any more.* FRANÇOISE *goes to the door and looks into the room.*]

They've killed him! They've killed him!

[*Absolute silence.* MAURICE *sits down, puts his head on the table. He is crying, perhaps. Silence. Long pause. Enter the two* EXECUTIONERS *with Jean, tied up as before. Jean is dead. His head hangs down inertly.*]

FRANÇOISE [*to the executioners*]: Let me see him. Let me see him properly.

[*The* EXECUTIONERS, *without paying any attention to Françoise, cross the room and go out by the street door.* FRANÇOISE *and* BENOÎT *sit down on either side of Maurice. They look at him. Silence.*]

MAURICE [*to Françoise*]: They killed Daddy because of you.

FRANÇOISE: How dare you say that to your mother? To your mother who has always taken so much trouble with you.

MAURICE [*interrupting her*]: Don't give me all that stuff. What I'm accusing you of is of denouncing Daddy.

[BENOÎT *is too depressed to intervene.*]

FRANÇOISE: Yes, my son, as you wish. If it gives you any pleasure I'll say it was my fault. Is that what you want?

MAURICE: Oh, stop harping on that. [*Pause. Long silence.*] Why did you treat Daddy like that, Daddy who never gave you anything to complain of?

FRANÇOISE: That's it. That's what I've been waiting for, all my life. When your father compromised the future of his children and his wife because of his. . . .

MAURICE [*interrupting her*]: What's all that stuff about compromising the future? What's your latest invention?

FRANÇOISE: Ah, my son! What misery! What a cross! [*Pause.*] Of course he compromised his children's future by his failings. He knew very well that if he continued in his guilty ways he would sooner or later finish up the way he has. He knew it only too well, but he didn't change, he continued, whatever happened, on his guilty way. How many times did I tell him so! How many times did I tell him: you're going to leave me a widow and your sons orphans. But what did he do? He ignored my advice and persisted in the error of his ways.

MAURICE: You're the only one who says he was guilty.

FRANÇOISE: Ah yes, naturally, you're not content now with having insulted me all night long, but you're going to call me a liar as well and swear that I make people perjure themselves. That's the way you treat a mother who, ever since you were born, has given you all her care and attention. While your father was compromising your future with his misbehaviour, I was thinking of your happiness and I had only one aim – to make you happy, to give you all the happiness that I had never known. Because for me, the only thing that counts is that your brother and you should be all right, everything else was of no importance. I'm a poor, ignorant, uneducated woman, who wants nothing but the good of her children, whatever the cost.

BENOÎT [*conciliatingly*]: Maurice, there isn't any point in making a fuss now; Daddy's dead, we can't do anything about it now.

FRANÇOISE: Benoît's right.

[*Long silence.*]

MAURICE: We could have prevented Daddy's death.

FRANÇOISE: How? Was it my fault? No. He was the one who was guilty – he, your father. What could I do? What could I do to stop him being like that? He'd got stubborn. I'm only a poor, ignorant, uneducated woman, I've spent my whole life doing nothing but worrying about other people, forgetting myself. When have you seen me buy a pretty dress or go to the cinema or to first nights, which I used to like so much? No, I didn't do any of those things, in spite of all the pleasure I'd have got out of them, and that was only because I preferred to devote myself entirely to you. I only ask one thing – that you shouldn't be ungrateful, and that you should be capable of appreciating the sacrifice of a mother like the one you were lucky enough to have.

BENOÎT: Yes, Mother, *I* appreciate all you've done for us.

FRANÇOISE: Yes, I know *you* do, but your brother doesn't. It doesn't seem anything to your brother, it isn't enough for him. How happy we could be if only we were all united, if only we all agreed!

BENOÎT: Maurice, yes, we ought to understand one another and all three live in peace. Mother is very good, I know she loves you very much and that she'll give you everything you need. Even if it's only out of selfishness, come back to us. We'll all three live happily and joyfully together and love one another.

MAURICE: But ... [*Pause.*] Daddy ...

[*Silence.*]

BENOÎT: That's already past history. Don't look backwards. What matters is the future. It would be too stupid to hang on to the past. You'll have everything you want with mother. Everything that's hers will be yours. Isn't that so, Mother?

FRANÇOISE: Yes, my son, everything that is mine will be his; I forgive him.

BENOÎT: You see how good she is; she even forgives you.

FRANÇOISE: Yes, I forgive you, and I shall forget all your insults.

BENOÎT: She'll forget everything! [*Gaily*] That's the important thing. And so we'll all three live together without ill-feeling; Mother, you, and me. What could be more wonderful?

MAURICE [*half convinced*]: Yes, but ...

BENOÎT [*interrupting him*]: No, you mustn't be vindictive. Be like Mother. She has reason to be angry with you, but she's promised to forget everything. We shall be happy if you'll be nice.

[MAURICE, *full of emotion, lowers his head. Long silence.* BENOÎT *puts his arm round his brother.*]

Kiss Mother.

[*Silence.*]

Kiss her and let bygones be bygones.

[MAURICE *goes up to his mother and kisses her.*]

FRANÇOISE: My son!

BENOÎT [*to Maurice*]: Ask Mother to forgive you.

MAURICE [*nearly crying*] : Forgive me, Mother.
  [MAURICE *and* FRANÇOISE *embrace.* BENOÎT *joins them
  and all three stay enfolded in each others' arms while the curtain
  falls.*]

CURTAIN

EDWARD ALBEE

THE ZOO STORY

A Play in One Scene

for

William Flanagan

THE ZOO STORY

First performed on 28 September 1959, at the Schiller Theatre Werkstatt, Berlin

CHARACTERS

PETER: A man in his early forties, neither fat nor gaunt, neither handsome nor homely. He wears tweeds, smokes a pipe, carries horn-rimmed glasses. Although he is moving into middle age, his dress and his manner would suggest a man younger.

JERRY: A man in his late thirties, not poorly dressed, but carelessly. What was once a trim and lightly muscled body has begun to go to fat; and while he is no longer handsome, it is evident that he once was. His fall from physical grace should not suggest debauchery; he has, to come closest to it, a great weariness.

It is Central Park; a Sunday afternoon in summer; the present. There are two park benches, one towards either side of the stage; they both face the audience. Behind them: foliage, trees, sky. At the beginning, PETER *is seated on one of the benches.*

> [*As the curtain rises,* PETER *is seated on the bench stage-right. He is reading a book. He stops reading, cleans his glasses, goes back to reading.* JERRY *enters.*]

JERRY: I've been to the zoo. [PETER *doesn't notice.*] I said, I've been to the zoo. MISTER, I'VE BEEN TO THE ZOO!

PETER: Hm? . . . What? . . . I'm sorry, were you talking to me?

JERRY: I went to the zoo, and then I walked until I came here. Have I been walking north?

PETER [*puzzled*]: North? Why . . . I . . . I think so. Let me see.

JERRY [*pointing past the audience*]: Is that Fifth Avenue?

PETER: Why yes; yes, it is.

JERRY: And what is that cross street there; that one, to the right?

PETER: That? Oh, that's Seventy-fourth Street.

JERRY: And the zoo is around Sixty-fifth Street; so, I've been walking north.

PETER [*anxious to get back to his reading*]: Yes: it would seem so.

JERRY: Good old north.

PETER [*lightly, by reflex*]: Ha, ha.

JERRY [*after a slight pause*]: But not due north.

PETER: I . . . well, no, not due north; but, we . . . call it north. It's northerly.

JERRY [*watches as* PETER, *anxious to dismiss him, prepares his pipe*]: Well, boy; you're not going to get lung cancer, are you?

PETER [*looks up, a little annoyed, then smiles*]: No, sir. Not from this.

JERRY: No, sir. What you'll probably get is cancer of the mouth, and then you'll have to wear one of those things Freud wore after they took one whole side of his jaw away. What do they call those things?

PETER [*uncomfortable*]: A prosthesis?

JERRY: The very thing! A prosthesis. You're an educated man, aren't you? Are you a doctor?

PETER: Oh, no; no. I read about it somewhere: *Time* magazine, I think. [*He turns to his book.*]

JERRY: Well, *Time* magazine isn't for blockheads.

PETER: No, I suppose not.

JERRY [*after a pause*]: Boy, I'm glad that's Fifth Avenue there.

PETER [*vaguely*]: Yes.

JERRY: I don't like the west side of the park much.

PETER: Oh? [*then, slightly wary, but interested*] Why?

JERRY [*off-hand*]: I don't know.

PETER: Oh. [*He returns to his book.*]

JERRY [*stands for a few seconds, looking at* PETER, *who finally looks up again, puzzled*]: Do you mind if we talk?

PETER [*obviously minding*]: Why . . . no, no.

JERRY: Yes you do; you do.

PETER [*puts his book down, his pipe out and away, smiling*]: No, really; I don't mind.

JERRY: Yes you do.

PETER [*finally decided*]: No; I don't mind at all, really.

JERRY: It's . . . it's a nice day.

PETER [*stares unnecessarily at the sky*]: Yes. Yes, it is; lovely.

JERRY: I've been to the zoo.

PETER: Yes, I think you said so . . . didn't you?

JERRY: You'll read about it in the papers tomorrow, if you don't see it on your TV tonight. You have TV, haven't you?

PETER: Why yes, we have two; one for the children.

JERRY: You're married!

PETER [*with pleased emphasis*]: Why, certainly.

JERRY: It isn't a law, for God's sake.

PETER: No . . . no, of course not.

JERRY: And you have a wife.

PETER [*bewildered by the seeming lack of communication*]: Yes!

JERRY: And you have children.

PETER: Yes; two.

JERRY: Boys?

PETER: No, girls ... both girls.

JERRY: But you wanted boys.

PETER: Well ... naturally, every man wants a son, but ...

JERRY [*lightly mocking*]: But that's the way the cookie crumbles?

PETER [*annoyed*]: I wasn't going to say that.

JERRY: And you're not going to have any more kids, are you?

PETER [*a bit distantly*]: No. No more. [*Then back, and irksome*] Why did you say that? How would you know about that?

JERRY: The way you cross your legs, perhaps; something in the voice. Or maybe I'm just guessing. Is it your wife?

PETER [*furious*]: That's none of your business! [*A silence.*] Do you understand?

[JERRY *nods.* PETER *is quiet now.*]
Well, you're right. We'll have no more children.

JERRY [*softly*]: That *is* the way the cookie crumbles.

PETER [*forgiving*]: Yes ... I guess so.

JERRY: Well, now; what else?

PETER: What were you saying about the zoo ... that I'd read about it, or see ...?

JERRY: I'll tell you about it, soon. Do you mind if I ask you questions?

PETER: Oh, not really.

JERRY: I'll tell you why I do it; I don't talk to many people – except to say like: give me a beer, or where's the john, or what time does the feature go on, or keep your hands to yourself, buddy. You know – things like that.

PETER: I must say I don't ...

JERRY: But every once in a while I like to talk to somebody, really *talk*; like to get to know somebody, know all about him.

PETER [*lightly laughing, still a little uncomfortable*]: And am I the guinea pig for today?

JERRY: On a sun-drenched Sunday afternoon like this: Who better than a nice married man with two daughters and . . . uh . . . a dog?

[PETER *shakes his head.*]

No? Two dogs.

[PETER *shakes his head again.*]

Hm. No dogs?

[PETER *shakes his head, sadly.*]

Oh, that's a shame. But you look like an animal man. CATS?

[PETER *nods his head, ruefully.*]

Cats! But, that can't be your idea. No, sir. Your wife and daughters?

[PETER *nods his head.*]

Is there anything else I should know?

PETER [*has to clear his throat*]: There are . . . there are two parakeets. One . . . uh . . . one for each of my daughters.

JERRY: Birds.

PETER: My daughters keep them in a cage in their bedroom.

JERRY: Do they carry disease? The birds.

PETER: I don't believe so.

JERRY: That's too bad. If they did you could set them loose in the house and the cats could eat them and die, maybe.

[PETER *looks blank for a moment, then laughs.*]

And what else? What do you do to support your enormous household?

PETER: I . . . uh . . . I have an executive position with a . . . a small publishing house. We . . . uh . . . we publish text-books.

JERRY: That sounds nice; very nice. What do you make?

PETER [*still cheerful*]: Now look here!

JERRY: Oh, come on.

PETER: Well, I make around eighteen thousand a year, but I don't carry more than forty dollars at any one time . . . in case you're a . . . a holdup man . . . ha, ha, ha.

JERRY [*ignoring the above*]: Where do you live?

[PETER *is reluctant.*]

Oh, look; I'm not going to rob you, and I'm not going to kidnap your parakeets, your cats, or your daughters.

PETER [*too loud*]: I live between Lexington and Third Avenue, on Seventy-fourth Street.

JERRY: That wasn't so hard, was it?

PETER: I didn't mean to seem . . . ah . . . it's that you don't really carry on a conversation; you just ask questions. And I'm . . . I'm normally . . . uh . . . reticent. Why do you just stand there?

JERRY: I'll start walking around in a little while, and eventually I'll sit down. [*Recalling*] Wait until you see the expression on his face.

PETER: What? Whose face? Look here; is this something about the zoo?

JERRY [*distantly*]: The what?

PETER: The zoo; the zoo. Something about the zoo.

JERRY: The zoo?

PETER: You've mentioned it several times.

JERRY [*still distant, but returning abruptly*]: The zoo? Oh, yes; the zoo. I was there before I came here. I told you that. Say, what's the dividing line between upper-middle-middle-class and lower-upper-middle-class?

PETER: My dear fellow, I . . .

JERRY: Don't my dear fellow me.

PETER [*unhappily*]: Was I patronizing? I believe I was; I'm sorry. But, you see, your question about the classes bewildered me.

JERRY: And when you're bewildered you become patronizing?

PETER: I . . . I don't express myself too well, sometimes. [*He attempts a joke on himself.*] I'm in publishing, not writing.

JERRY [*amused, but not at the humour*]: So be it. The truth *is*: *I* was being patronizing.

PETER: Oh, now; you needn't say that.

[*It is at this point that* JERRY *may begin to move about the stage*

163

with slowly increasing determination and authority, but pacing himself, so that the long speech about the dog comes at the high point of the arc.]

JERRY: All right. Who are your favourite writers? Baudelaire and J. P. Marquand?

PETER [*wary*]: Well, I like a great many writers; I have a considerable ... catholicity of taste, if I may say so. Those two men are fine, each in his way. [*Warming up*] Baudelaire, of course ... uh ... is by far the finer of the two, but Marquand has a place ... in our ... uh ... national ...

JERRY: Skip it.

PETER: I ... sorry.

JERRY: Do you know what I did before I went to the zoo today? I walked all the way up Fifth Avenue from Washington Square; all the way.

PETER: Oh; you live in the Village! [*This seems to enlighten Peter.*]

JERRY: No, I don't. I took the subway down to the Village so I could walk all the way up Fifth Avenue to the zoo. It's one of those things a person has to do; sometimes a person has to go a very long distance out of his way to come back a short distance correctly.

PETER [*almost pouting*]: Oh, I thought you lived in the Village.

JERRY: What were you trying to do? Make sense out of things? Bring order? The old pigeonhole bit? Well, that's easy; I'll tell you. I live in a four-storey brownstone rooming-house on the upper West Side between Columbus Avenue and Central Park West. I live on the top floor; rear; west. It's a laughably small room, and one of my walls is made of beaverboard; this beaverboard separates my room from another laughably small room, so I assume that the two rooms were once one room, a small room, but not necessarily laughable. The room beyond my beaverboard wall is occupied by a coloured queen who always keeps his door open; well, not always but *always* when he's plucking his eyebrows, which he does with Buddhist concentration.

This coloured queen has rotten teeth, which is rare, and he has a Japanese kimono, which is also pretty rare; and he wears this kimono to and from the john in the hall, which is pretty frequent. I mean, he goes to the john a lot. He never bothers me, and never brings anyone up to his room. All he does is pluck his eyebrows, wear his kimono and go to the john. Now, the two front rooms on my floor are a little larger, I guess; but they're pretty small, too. There's a Puerto Rican family in one of them, a husband, a wife, and some kids; I don't know how many. These people entertain a lot. And in the other front room, there's somebody living there, but I don't know who it is. I've never seen who it is. Never. Never ever.

PETER [*embarrassed*]: Why . . . why do you live there?

JERRY [*from a distance again*]: I don't know.

PETER: It doesn't sound a very nice place . . . where you live.

JERRY: Well, no; it isn't an apartment in the East Seventies. But, then again, I don't have one wife, two daughters, two cats and two parakeets. What I do have, I have toilet articles, a few clothes, a hot plate that I'm not supposed to have, a can opener, one that works with a key, you know: a knife, two forks, and two spoons, one small, one large; three plates, a cup, a saucer, a drinking glass, two picture frames, both empty, eight or nine books, a pack of pornographic playing-cards, regular deck, an old Western Union typewriter that prints nothing but capital letters, and a small strong-box without a lock which has in it . . . what? Rocks! Some rocks . . . sea-rounded rocks I picked up on the beach when I was a kid. Under which . . . weighed down . . . are some letters . . . please letters . . . please why don't you do this, and please when will you do that letters. And when letters, too. When will you write? When will you come? When? These letters are from more recent years.

PETER [*stares glumly at his shoes, then –*]: About those two empty picture frames . . . ?

JERRY: I don't see why they need any explanation at all. Isn't it clear? I don't have pictures of anyone to put in them.

PETER: Your parents ... perhaps ... a girl-friend ...

JERRY: You're a very sweet man, and you're possessed of a truly enviable innocence. But good old Mom and good old Pop are dead ... you know? ... I'm broken up about it, too ... I mean really. BUT. That particular vaudeville act is playing the cloud circuit now, so I don't see how I can look at them, all neat and framed. Besides, or, rather, to be pointed about it, good old Mom walked out on good old Pop when I was ten and a half years old; she embarked on an adulterous turn of our southern states ... a journey of a year's duration ... and her most constant companion ... among others, among many others ... was a Mr Barleycorn. At least, that's what good old Pop told me after he went down ... came back ... brought her body north. We'd received the news between Christmas and New Year's, you see, that good old Mom had parted with the ghost in some dump in Alabama. And, without the ghost ... she was less welcome. I mean, what was she? A stiff ... a northern stiff. At any rate, good old Pop celebrated the New Year for an even two weeks and then slapped into the front of a somewhat moving city omnibus, which sort of cleaned things out family-wise. Well no; then there was Mom's sister, who was given neither to sin nor the consolations of the bottle. I moved in on her, and my memory of her is slight excepting I remember still that she did all things dourly: sleeping, eating, working, praying. She dropped dead on the stairs to her apartment, my apartment then, too, on the afternoon of my high school graduation. A terribly middle-European joke, if you ask me.

PETER: Oh, my; oh, my.

JERRY: Oh, your what? But that was a long time ago, and I have no feeling about any of it that I care to admit to myself. Perhaps you can see, though, why good old Mom and good old Pop are frameless. What's your name? Your first name?

PETER: I'm Peter.

JERRY: I'd forgotten to ask you. I'm Jerry.

PETER [*with a slight nervous laugh*]: Hello, Jerry.

JERRY [*nods his hello*]: And let's see now; what's the point of having a girl's picture, especially in two frames? I have two picture frames, you remember. I never see the pretty little ladies more than once, and most of them wouldn't be caught in the same room with a camera. It's odd, and I wonder if it's sad.

PETER: The girls?

JERRY: No. I wonder if it's sad that I never see the little ladies more than once. I've never been able to have sex with, or, how is it put? . . . make love to anybody more than once. Once; that's it . . . Oh, wait; for a week and a half, when I was fifteen . . . and I hang my head in shame that puberty was late . . . I was a h-o-m-o-s-e-x-u-a-l. I mean, I was queer . . . [*Very fast*] . . . queer, queer, queer . . . with bells ringing, banners snapping in the wind. And for those eleven days, I met at least twice a day with the park superinten-dent's son . . . a Greek boy, whose birthday was the same as mine, except he was a year older. I think I was very much in love . . . maybe just with sex. But that was the jazz of a very special hotel, wasn't it? And now; oh, do I love the little ladies; really, I love them. For about an hour.

PETER: Well, it seems perfectly simple to me . . .

JERRY [*angry*]: Look! Are you going to tell me to get married and have parakeets?

PETER [*angry himself*]: Forget the parakeets! And stay single if you want to. It's no business of mine. I didn't start this conversation in the . . .

JERRY: All right, all right. I'm sorry. All right? You're not angry?

PETER [*laughing*]: No, I'm not angry.

JERRY [*relieved*]: Good. [*Now back to his previous tone*] Interest-ing that you asked me about the picture frames. I would have thought that you would have asked me about the pornographic playing-cards.

PETER [*with a knowing smile*]: Oh, I've seen those cards.

JERRY: That's not the point. [*Laughs*] I suppose when you were a kid you and your pals passed them around, or you had a pack of your own.

PETER: Well, I guess a lot of us did.

JERRY: And you threw them away just before you got married.

PETER: Oh, now; look here. I didn't *need* anything like that when I got older.

JERRY: No?

PETER [*embarrassed*]: I'd rather not talk about these things.

JERRY: So? Don't. Besides, I wasn't trying to plumb your post-adolescent sexual life and hard times; what I wanted to get at is the value difference between pornographic playing-cards when you're a kid, and pornographic playing-cards when you're older. It's that when you're a kid you use the cards as a substitute for a real experience, and when you're older you use real experience as a substitute for the fantasy. But I imagine you'd rather hear about what happened at the zoo.

PETER [*enthusiastic*]: Oh, yes; the zoo. [*Then awkward*] That is . . . if you . . .

JERRY: Let me tell you about why I went . . . well, let me tell you some things. I've told you about the fourth floor of the rooming-house where I live. I think the rooms are better as you go down, floor by floor. I guess they are; I don't know. I don't know any of the people on the third and second floors. Oh, wait! I do know that there's a lady living on the third floor, in the front. I know because she cries all the time. Whenever I go out or come back in, whenever I pass her door, I always hear her crying, muffled, but . . . very determined. Very determined indeed. But the one I'm getting to, and all about the dog, is the landlady. I don't like to use words that are too harsh in describing people. I don't like to. But the landlady is a fat, ugly, mean, stupid, unwashed, misanthropic, cheap, drunken bag of garbage. And you may have noticed that I very seldom use profanity, so I can't describe her as well as I might.

PETER: You describe her . . . vividly.

JERRY: Well, thanks. Anyway, she has a dog, and I will tell you about the dog, and she and her dog are the gate-keepers of my dwelling. The woman is bad enough; she leans around in the entrance hall, spying to see that I don't bring in things or people, and when she's had her mid-afternoon pint of lemon-flavoured gin she always stops me in the hall, and grabs ahold of my coat or my arm, and she presses her disgusting body up against me to keep me in a corner so she can talk to me. The smell of her body and her breath . . . you can't imagine it . . . and somewhere, some-where in the back of that pea-sized brain of hers, an organ developed just enough to let her eat, drink and emit, she has some foul parody of sexual desire. And I, Peter, I am the object of her sweaty lust.

PETER: That's disgusting. That's . . . horrible.

JERRY: But I have found a way to keep her off. When she talks to me, when she presses herself to my body and mum-bles about her room and how I should come there, I merely say: but, Love; wasn't yesterday enough for you, and the day before? Then she puzzles, she makes slits of her tiny eyes, she sways a little, and then, Peter . . . and it is at this moment that I think I might be doing some good in that tormented house . . . a simple-minded smile begins to form on her unthinkable face, and she giggles and groans as she thinks about yesterday and the day before; as she believes and relives what never happened. Then, she motions to that black monster of a dog she has, and she goes back to her room. And I am safe until our next meeting.

PETER: It's so . . . unthinkable. I find it hard to believe that people such as that really *are*.

JERRY [*lightly mocking*]: It's for reading about, isn't it?

PETER [*seriously*]: Yes.

JERRY: And fact is better left to fiction. You're right, Peter. Well, what I have been meaning to tell you about is the dog; I shall, now.

PETER [*nervously*]: Oh, yes; the dog.

JERRY: Don't go. You're not thinking of going, are you?

PETER: Well . . . no, I don't think so.

JERRY [*as if to a child*]: Because after I tell you about the dog, do you know what then? Then . . . then I'll tell you about what happened at the zoo.

PETER [*laughing faintly*]: You're . . . you're full of stories, aren't you?

JERRY: You don't *have* to listen. Nobody is holding you here; remember that. Keep that in your mind.

PETER [*irritably*]: I know that.

JERRY: You do? Good.

[*The following long speech, it seems to me, should be done with a great deal of action, to achieve a hypnotic effect on Peter, and on the audience too. Some specific actions have been suggested, but the director and the actor playing Jerry might best work it out for themselves.*]

ALL RIGHT. [*As if reading from a huge bill-board*] THE STORY OF JERRY AND THE DOG! [*Natural again*] What I am going to tell you has something to do with how sometimes it's necessary to go a long distance out of the way in order to come back a short distance correctly; or, maybe I only think that it has something to do with that. But, it's why I went to the zoo today, and why I walked north . . . northerly, rather . . . until I came here. All right. The dog, I think I told you, is a black monster of a beast: an oversized head, tiny, tiny ears, and eyes . . . bloodshot, infected, maybe; and a body you can see the ribs through the skin. The dog is black, all black; all black except for the bloodshot eyes, and . . . yes . . . and an open sore on its . . . *right* forepaw; that is red, too. And, oh yes; the poor monster, and I do believe it's an old dog . . . it's certainly a misused one . . . almost always has an erection . . . of sorts. That's red, too. And . . . what else? . . . oh, yes; there's a greyyellow-white colour, too, when he bares his fangs. Like this: Grrrrrrr! Which is what he did when he saw me for the first time . . . the day I moved in. I worried about that animal the very first minute I met him. Now, animals don't take to me like Saint Francis had birds hanging off him all the time. What I mean is: animals are indifferent to me . . . like people [*He smiles slightly*] . . . most of the time. But this dog wasn't indifferent. From the very beginning he'd snarl and then go for me, to get one of my legs. Not like he was rabid, you know; he was sort of a stumbly dog, but he wasn't half-assed, either. It was a good, stumbly run; but I always got away. He got a piece of my trouser leg, look, you can see right here, where it's mended; he got that the second day I lived there; but, I kicked free and got upstairs fast, so that was that. [*Puzzles*] I still don't know to this day how the other roomers manage it, but you know what I *think*: I think it had to do only with me. Cosy. So. Anyway, this went on for over a week, whenever I came in; but never when I went out. That's funny. Or, it *was* funny. I could pack up and live in the street for all the dog cared. Well, I thought about it up in my room one day, one of the times after I'd bolted upstairs, and I made up my mind. I decided: First, I'll kill the dog with kindness, and if that doesn't work . . . I'll just kill him.

[PETER *winces*.]

Don't react, Peter; just listen. So, the next day I went out and bought a bag of hamburgers, medium rare, no catsup, no onion; and on the way home I threw away all the rolls and kept just the meat.

[*Action for the following, perhaps.*]

When I got back to the rooming-house the dog was waiting for me. I half opened the door that led into the entrance hall, and there he was; waiting for me. It figures. I went in, very cautiously, and I had the hamburgers, you remember; I opened the bag, and I set the meat down about twelve feet from where the dog was snarling at me. Like so! He snarled; stopped snarling; sniffed; moved slowly; then faster; then faster towards the meat. Well, when he got to it he stopped, and he looked at me. I smiled; but tentatively, you understand. He turned his face back to the hamburgers, smelled, sniffed some more, and then . . .

RRRAAAAGGGGGHHHH, like that . . . he tore into them.
It was as if he had never eaten anything in his life before,
except like garbage. Which might very well have been the
truth. I don't think the landlady ever eats anything but
garbage. But. He ate all the hamburgers, almost all at
once, making sounds in his throat like a woman. Then
when he'd finished the meat, the hamburger, and tried to
eat the paper, too, he sat down and smiled. I think he
smiled; I know cats do. It was a very gratifying few
moments. Then, BAM, he snarled and made for me again.
He didn't get me this time, either. So, I got upstairs, and I
lay down on my bed and started to think about the dog
again. To be truthful, I was offended, and I was damn mad,
too. It was six perfectly good hamburgers with not enough
pork in them to make it disgusting. I was offended. But,
after a while, I decided to try it for a few more days. If you
think about it, this dog had what amounted to an antipathy
towards me; really. And, I wondered if I mightn't overcome this antipathy. So, I tried it for five more days, but it
was always the same: snarl, sniff; move; faster; stare;
gobble; RAAGGGHHH; smile; snarl; BAM. Well, now; by
this time Columbus Avenue was strewn with hamburger
rolls and I was less offended than disgusted. So, I decided
to kill the dog.

[PETER *raises a hand in protest.*]

Oh, don't be so alarmed, Peter; I didn't succeed. The day
I tried to kill the dog I bought only one hamburger and
what I thought was a murderous portion of rat poison.
When I bought the hamburger I asked the man not to
bother with the roll, all I wanted was the meat. I expected
some reaction from him, like: we don't sell no hamburgers
without rolls; or, wha' d'ya wanna do, eat it out'a ya
han's? But no; he smiled benignly, wrapped up the hamburger in waxed paper, and said: A bite for ya pussy-cat?
I wanted to say: No, not really; it's part of a plan to poison
a dog I know. But, you can't say 'a dog I know' without
sounding funny; so I said, a little too loud, I'm afraid, and

too formally: YES, A BITE FOR MY PUSSYCAT. People looked up. It always happens when I try to simplify things; people look up. But that's neither hither nor thither. So. On my way back to the rooming-house, I kneaded the hamburger and the rat poison together between my hands, at that point feeling as much sadness as disgust. I opened the door to the entrance hall, and there the monster was, waiting to take the offering and then jump me. Poor bastard; he never learned that the moment he took to smile before he went for me gave me time enough to get out of range. BUT, there he was; malevolence with an erection, waiting. I put the poison patty down, moved towards the stairs and watched. The poor animal gobbled the food down as usual, smiled, which made me almost sick, and then, BAM. But, I sprinted up the stairs, as usual, and the dog didn't get me, as usual. AND IT CAME TO PASS THAT THE BEAST WAS DEATHLY ILL. I knew this because he no longer attended me, and because the landlady sobered up. She stopped me in the hall the same evening of the attempted murder and confided the information that God had struck her puppydog a surely fatal blow. She had forgotten her bewildered lust, and her eyes were wide open for the first time. They looked like the dog's eyes. She snivelled and implored me to pray for the animal. I wanted to say to her: Madam, I have myself to pray for, the coloured queen, the Puerto Rican family, the person in the front room whom I've never seen, the woman who cries deliberately behind her closed door, and the rest of the people in all rooming-houses, everywhere; besides, Madam, I don't understand how to pray. But ... to simplify things ... I told her I would pray. She looked up. She said that I was a liar, and that I probably wanted the dog to die. I told her, and there was so much truth here, that I didn't want the dog to die. I didn't, and not just because I'd poisoned him. I'm afraid that I must tell you I wanted the dog to live so that I could see what our new relationship might come to.

[PETER *indicates his increasing displeasure and slowly growing antagonism.*]

Please understand, Peter; that sort of thing is important
You must believe me; it *is* important. We have to know the
effect of our actions. [*Another deep sigh.*] Well, anyway; the
dog recovered. I have no idea why, unless he was a descen-
dant of the puppy that guarded the gates of hell or some
such resort. I'm not up on my mythology. [*He pronounces the
word myth-o-logy.*] Are you?

[PETER *sets to thinking, but* JERRY *goes on.*]

At any rate, and you've missed the eight-thousand-dollar
question, Peter; at any rate, the dog recovered his health
and the landlady recovered her thirst, in no way altered by
the bow-wow's deliverance. When I came home from a
movie that was playing on Forty-second Street, a movie
I'd seen, or one that was very much like one or several I'd
seen, after the landlady told me puppykins was better, I
was so hoping for the dog to be waiting for me. I was . . .
well, how would you put it . . . enticed? . . . fascinated? . . .
no, I don't think so . . . heart-shatteringly anxious, that's it: I
was heart-shatteringly anxious to confront my friend again.

[PETER *reacts scoffingly.*]

Yes, Peter; friend. That's the only word for it. I was heart-
shatteringly et cetera to confront my doggy friend again. I
came in the door and advanced, unafraid, to the centre of
the entrance hall. The beast was there . . . looking at me.
And, you know, he looked better for his scrape with the
nevermind. I stopped; I looked at him; he looked at me. I
think . . . I think we stayed a long time that way . . . still,
stone-statue . . . just looking at one another. I looked more
into his face than he looked into mine. I mean, I can concentrate longer at looking into a dog's face than a dog can
concentrate at looking into mine, or into anybody else's
face, for that matter. But during that twenty seconds or
two hours that we looked into each other's face, we made
contact. Now, here is what I had wanted to happen: I
loved the dog now, and I wanted him to love me. I had

tried to love, and I had tried to kill, and both had been unsuccessful by themselves. I hoped . . . and I don't really know why I expected the dog to understand anything, much less my motivations . . . I hoped that the dog would understand.

[PETER *seems to be hypnotized.*]

It's just . . . it's just that . . . [JERRY *is abnormally tense, now.*] . . . it's just that if you can't deal with people, you have to make a start somewhere. WITH ANIMALS! [*Much faster now, and like a conspirator*] Don't you see? A person has to have some way of dealing with SOMETHING. If not with people . . . SOMETHING. With a bed, with a cockroach, with a mirror . . . no, that's too hard, that's one of the last steps. With a cockroach, with a . . . with a . . . with a carpet, a roll of toilet paper . . . no, not that, either . . . that's a mirror, too; always check bleeding. You see how hard it is to find things? With a street corner, and too many lights, all colours reflecting on the oily-wet streets . . . with a wisp of smoke, a wisp . . . of smoke . . . with . . . with pornographic playing-cards, with a strong-box . . . WITHOUT A LOCK . . . with love, with vomiting, with crying, with fury because the pretty little ladies aren't pretty little ladies, with making money with your body which is an act of love and I could prove it, with howling because you're alive; with God. How about that? WITH GOD WHO IS A COLOURED QUEEN WHO WEARS A KIMONO AND PLUCKS HIS EYEBROWS! WHO IS A WOMAN WHO CRIES WITH DETERMINATION BEHIND HER CLOSED DOOR . . . with God who, I'm told, turned his back on the whole thing some time ago . . . with . . . some day, with people. [JERRY *sighs the next word heavily.*] People. With an idea; a concept. And where better, where ever better in this humiliating excuse for a jail, where better to communicate one single, simple-minded idea than in an entrance hall? Where? It would be A START! Where better to make a beginning . . . to understand and just possibly be understood . . . a beginning of an understanding, than with . . .

[*Here* JERRY *seems to fall into almost grotesque fatigue*] . . . than with A DOG. Just that; a dog. [*Here there is a silence that might be prolonged for a moment or so; then* JERRY *wearily finishes his story.*] A dog. It seemed like a perfectly sensible idea. Man is a dog's best friend, remember. So: the dog and I looked at each other. I longer than the dog. And what I saw then has been the same ever since. Whenever the dog and I see each other we both stop where we are. We regard each other with a mixture of sadness and suspicion, and then we feign indifference. We walk past each other safely; we have an understanding. It's very sad, but you'll have to admit that it is an understanding. We had made many attempts at contact, and we had failed. The dog has returned to garbage, and I to solitary but free passage. I have not returned. I mean to say, I have *gained* solitary free passage, if that much further loss can be said to be gain. I have learned that neither kindness nor cruelty by themselves, independent of each other, creates any effect beyond themselves; and I have learned that the two combined, together, at the same time, are the teaching emotion. And what is gained is loss. And what has been the result: the dog and I have attained a compromise; more of a bargain, really. We neither love nor hurt because we do not try to reach each other. And, *was* trying to feed the dog an act of love? And, perhaps, was the dog's attempt to bite me *not* an act of love? If we can so misunderstand, well then, why have we invented the word love in the first place?

[*There is silence.* JERRY *moves to Peter's bench and sits down beside him. This is the first time Jerry has sat down during the play.*]

The Story of Jerry and the Dog: the end.

[PETER *is silent.*]

Well, Peter? [JERRY *is suddenly cheerful.*] Well, Peter? Do you think I could sell that story to the *Reader's Digest* and make a couple of hundred bucks for *The Most Unforgettable Character I've Ever Met*? Huh?

[JERRY *is animated, but* PETER *is disturbed.*]

Oh, come on now, Peter; tell me what you think.

PETER [*numb*]: I . . . I don't understand what . . . I don't think I . . . [*Now almost tearfully*] Why did you tell me all of this?

JERRY: Why not?

PETER: I DON'T UNDERSTAND!

JERRY [*furious, but whispering*]: That's a lie.

PETER: No. No, it's not.

JERRY [*quietly*]: I tried to explain it to you as I went along. I went slowly; it all has to do with . . .

PETER: I DON'T WANT TO HEAR ANY MORE. I don't understand you, or your landlady, or her dog. . . .

JERRY: *Her* dog! I thought it was my . . . No. No, you're right. It *is* her dog. [*Looks at* PETER *intently, shaking his head.*] I don't know what I was thinking about; of course you don't understand. [*In a monotone, wearily*] I don't live in your block; I'm not married to two parakeets, or whatever your set-up is. I am a *permanent transient*, and my home is the sickening rooming-houses on the West Side of New York City, which is the greatest city in the world. Amen.

PETER: I'm . . . I'm sorry; I didn't mean to . . .

JERRY: Forget it. I suppose you don't quite know what to make of me, eh?

PETER [*a joke*]: We get all kinds in publishing. [*Chuckles.*]

JERRY: You're a funny man. [*He forces a laugh.*] You know that? You're a very . . . a richly comic person.

PETER [*modestly, but amused*]: Oh, now, not really. [*Still chuckling.*]

JERRY: Peter, do I annoy you, or confuse you?

PETER [*lightly*]: Well, I must confess that this wasn't the kind of afternoon I'd anticipated.

JERRY: You mean, I'm not the gentleman you were expecting.

PETER: I wasn't expecting anybody.

JERRY: No, I don't imagine you were. But I'm here, and I'm not leaving.

PETER [*consulting his watch*]: Well, you may not be, but I must be getting home soon.

JERRY: Oh, come on; stay a while longer.

PETER: I really should get home; you see . . .

JERRY [*tickles Peter's ribs with his fingers*]. Oh, come on.

[PETER *is very ticklish; as* JERRY *continues to tickle him his voice becomes falsetto.*]

PETER: No, I . . . OHHHHH! Don't do that. Stop, Stop. Ohhh, no, no.

JERRY: Oh, come on.

PETER [*as* JERRY *tickles*]: Oh, hee, hee, hee. I must go. I . . . hee, hee, hee. After all, stop, stop, hee, hee, hee, after all, the parakeets will be getting dinner ready soon. Hee, hee. And the cats are setting the table. Stop, stop, and, and . . . [*He is beside himself now.*] . . . and we're having . . . hee, hee . . . uh . . . ho, ho, ho.

[JERRY *stops tickling Peter, but the combination of the tickling and his own mad whimsy has* PETER *laughing almost hysterically. As his laughter continues, then subsides,* JERRY *watches him, with a curious fixed smile.*]

JERRY: Peter?

PETER: Oh, ha, ha, ha, ha, ha. What? What?

JERRY: Listen, now.

PETER: Oh, ho, ho. What . . . what is it, Jerry? Oh, my.

JERRY [*mysteriously*]: Peter, do you want to know what happened at the zoo?

PETER: Ah, ha, ha. The what? Oh, yes; the zoo. Oh, ho, ho. Well, I had my own zoo there for a moment with . . . hee, hee, the parakeets getting dinner ready, and the . . . ha, ha, whatever it was, the . . .

JERRY [*calmly*]: Yes, that was very funny, Peter. I wouldn't have expected it. But do you want to hear about what happened at the zoo, or not?

PETER: Yes. Yes, by all means; tell me what happened at the zoo. Oh, my. I don't know what happened to me.

JERRY: Now I'll let you in on what happened at the zoo; but first, I should tell you why I went to the zoo. I went to the zoo to find out more about the way people exist with animals, and the way animals exist with each other, and with people too. It probably wasn't a fair test, what with everyone separated by bars from everyone else, the animals for the most part from each other, and always the people from the animals. But, if it's a zoo, that's the way it is. [*He pokes Peter on the arm.*] Move over.

PETER [*friendly*]: I'm sorry, haven't you enough room? [*He shifts a little.*]

JERRY [*smiling slightly*]: Well, all the animals are there, and all the people are there, and it's Sunday and all the children are there. [*He pokes Peter again.*] Move over.

PETER [*patiently, still friendly*]: All right.
　　[*He moves some more, and* JERRY *has all the room he might need.*]

JERRY: And it's a hot day, so all the stench is there, too, and all the balloon sellers, and all the ice-cream sellers, and all the seals are barking, and all the birds are screaming. [*Pokes Peter harder.*] Move over!

PETER [*beginning to be annoyed*]: Look here, you have more than enough room! [*But he moves more, and is now fairly cramped at one end of the bench.*]

JERRY: And I am there, and it's feeding time at the lion's house, and the lion keeper comes into the lion cage, one of the lion cages, to feed one of the lions. [*Punches Peter on the arm, hard.*] MOVE OVER!

PETER [*very annoyed*]: I can't move over any more, and stop hitting me. What's the matter with you?

JERRY: Do you want to hear the story? [*Punches Peter's arm again.*]

PETER [*flabbergasted*]: I'm not so sure! I certainly don't want to be punched in the arm.

JERRY [*punches Peter's arm again*]: Like that?

PETER: Stop it. What's the matter with you?

JERRY: I'm crazy, you bastard.

PETER: That isn't funny.

JERRY: Listen to me, Peter. I want this bench. You go sit on the bench over there, and if you're good I'll tell you the rest of the story.

PETER [*flustered*]: But . . . what ever for? What *is* the matter with you? Besides, I see no reason why I should give up this bench. I sit on this bench almost every Sunday afternoon, in good weather. It's secluded here; there's never anyone sitting here, so I have it all to myself.

JERRY [*softly*]: Get off this bench, Peter; I want it.

PETER [*almost whining*]: No.

JERRY: I said I want this bench, and I'm going to have it. Now get over there.

PETER: People can't have everything they want. You should know that; it's a rule; people can have some of the things they want, but they can't have everything.

JERRY [*laughs*]: Imbecile! You're slow-witted!

PETER: Stop that!

JERRY: You're a vegetable! Go lie down on the ground.

PETER [*intense*]: Now *you* listen to me. I've put up with you all afternoon.

JERRY: Not really.

PETER: LONG ENOUGH. I've put up with you long enough. I've listened to you because you seemed . . . well, because I thought you wanted to talk to somebody.

JERRY: You put things well; economically, and, yet . . . oh, what is the word I want to put justice to your . . . JESUS, you make me sick . . . get off here and give me my bench.

PETER: MY BENCH!

JERRY [*pushes Peter almost, but not quite, off the bench*]: Get out of my sight.

PETER [*regaining his position*]: God da . . . mn you. That's enough! I've had enough of you. I will not give up this bench; you can't have it, and that's that. Now, go away.

[JERRY *snorts but does not move.*]

Go away, I said.

[JERRY *does not move.*]

Get away from here. If you don't move on . . . you're a

180

bum . . . that's what you are. . . . If you don't move on, I'll get a policeman here and make you go.

[JERRY *laughs, stays.*]

I warn you, I'll call a policeman.

JERRY [*softly*]: You won't find a policeman around here; they're all over on the west side of the park chasing fairies down from trees or out of the bushes. That's all they do. That's their function. So scream your head off; it won't do you any good.

PETER: POLICE! I warn you, I'll have you arrested. POLICE! [*Pause.*] I said POLICE! [*Pause.*] I feel ridiculous.

JERRY: You look ridiculous: a grown man screaming for the police on a bright Sunday afternoon in the park with nobody harming you. If a policeman *did* fill his quota and come sludging over this way he'd probably take you in as a nut.

PETER [*with disgust and impotence*]: Great God, I just came here to read, and now you want me to give up the bench. You're mad.

JERRY: Hey, I got news for you, as they say. I'm on your precious bench, and you're never going to have it for yourself again.

PETER [*furious*]: Look, you; get off my bench. I don't care if it makes any sense or not. I want this bench to myself; I want you OFF IT!

JERRY [*mocking*]: Aw . . . look who's mad.

PETER: GET OUT!

JERRY: No.

PETER: I WARN YOU!

JERRY: Do you know how ridiculous you look *now*?

PETER [*his fury and self-consciousness have possessed him*]: It doesn't matter. [*He is almost crying.*] GET AWAY FROM MY BENCH!

JERRY: Why? You have everything in the world you want; you've told me about your home, and your family, and *your own* little zoo. You have everything, and now you want this bench. Are these the things men fight for? Tell me, Peter, is this bench, this iron and this wood, is this your honour? Is this the thing in the world you'd fight for? Can you think of anything more absurd?

PETER: Absurd? Look, I'm not going to talk to you about honour, or even try to explain it to you. Besides, it isn't a question of honour; but even if it were, you wouldn't understand.

JERRY [*contemptuously*]: You don't even know what you're saying, do you? This is probably the first time in your life you've had anything more trying to face than changing your cats' toilet box. Stupid! Don't you have any idea, not even the slightest, what other people *need*?

PETER: Oh, boy, listen to you; well, you don't need this bench. That's for sure.

JERRY: Yes; yes, I do.

PETER [*quivering*]: I've come here for years; I have hours of great pleasure, great satisfaction, right here. And that's important to a man. I'm a responsible person, and I'm a GROWN-UP. This is my bench, and you have no right to take it away from me.

JERRY: Fight for it, then. Defend yourself; defend your bench.

PETER: You've *pushed* me to it. Get up and fight.

JERRY: Like a man?

PETER [*still angry*]: Yes, like a man, if you insist on mocking me even further.

JERRY: I'll have to give you credit for one thing: you *are* a vegetable, and a slightly near-sighted one, I think ...

PETER: THAT'S ENOUGH. ...

JERRY: ... but, you know, as they say on TV all the time — you know — and I mean this, Peter, you have a certain dignity; it surprises me. ...

PETER: STOP!

JERRY [*rises lazily*]: Very well, Peter, we'll battle for the bench, but we're not evenly matched. [*He takes out and clicks open an ugly-looking knife.*]

PETER [*suddenly awakening to the reality of the situation*]: You *are*

mad! You're stark raving mad! YOU'RE GOING TO KILL
ME!

[*But before Peter has time to think what to do,* JERRY *tosses the
knife at Peter's feet.*]

JERRY: There you go. Pick it up. You have the knife and
we'll be more evenly matched.

PETER [*horrified*]: No!

[JERRY *rushes over to Peter, grabs him by the collar;* PETER
rises; their faces almost touch.]

JERRY: Now you pick up that knife and you fight with me.
You fight for your self-respect; you fight for that god-
damned bench.

PETER [*struggling*]: No! Let . . . let go of me! He . . . Help!

JERRY [*slaps Peter on each 'fight'*]: You fight, you miserable
bastard; fight for that bench; fight for your parakeets; fight
for your cats; fight for your two daughters; fight for your
wife; fight for your manhood, you pathetic little vegetable.
[*Spits in Peter's face*] You couldn't even get your wife with a
male child.

PETER [*breaks away, enraged*]: It's a matter of genetics, not
manhood, you . . . you monster. [*He darts down, picks up the
knife and backs off a little; breathing heavily.*] I'll give you one
last chance; get out of here and leave me alone! [*He holds
the knife with a firm arm, but far in front of him, not to attack, but
to defend.*]

JERRY [*sighs heavily*]: So be it!

[*With a rush he charges Peter and impales himself on the knife.
Tableau: For just a moment, complete silence, Jerry impaled on
the knife at the end of Peter's still firm arm. Then* PETER
screams, pulls away, leaving the knife in Jerry. JERRY *is
motionless, on point. Then he, too, screams, and it must be the
sound of an infuriated and fatally wounded animal. With the
knife in him, he stumbles back to the bench that Peter had
vacated. He crumbles there, sitting, facing Peter, his eyes wide
in agony, his mouth open.*]

PETER [*whispering*]: Oh my God, oh my God, oh my God . . .

[PETER *repeats these words many times, very rapidly.* JERRY *is dying; but now his expression seems to change. His features relax, and while his voice varies, sometimes wrenched with pain, for the most part he seems removed from his dying. He smiles.*]

JERRY: Thank you, Peter. I mean that, now; thank you very much.

[PETER's *mouth drops open. He cannot move; he is transfixed.*] Oh, Peter, I was so afraid I'd drive you away. [*He laughs as best he can.*] You don't know how afraid I was you'd go away and leave me. And now I'll tell you what happened at the zoo. I think . . . I think this is what happened at the zoo . . . I think. I think that while I was at the zoo I decided that I would walk north . . . northerly, rather . . . until I found you . . . or somebody . . . and I decided that I would talk to you . . . I would tell you things . . . and things that I would tell you would . . . Well, here we are. You see? Here we *are*. But . . . I don't know . . . could I have planned all this? No . . . no, I couldn't have. But I think I did. And now I've told you what you wanted to know, haven't I? And now you know all about what happened at the zoo. And now you know what you'll see in your TV, and the face I told you about . . . you remember . . . the face I told you about . . . my face, the face you see right now. Peter . . . Peter? . . . Peter . . . thank you. I came unto you [*He laughs, so faintly.*] and you have comforted me. Dear Peter.

PETER [*almost fainting*]: Oh my God!

JERRY: You'd better go now. Somebody might come by, and you don't want to be here when anyone comes.

PETER [*does not move, but begins to weep*]: Oh my God, oh my God.

JERRY [*most faintly, now; he is very near death*]: You won't be coming back here any more, Peter; you've been dispossessed. You've lost your bench, but you've defended your honour. And Peter, I'll tell you something now; you're not really a vegetable; it's all right, you're an animal. You're an animal, too. But you'd better hurry now, Peter. Hurry, you'd better go . . . see? [JERRY *takes a handkerchief and with great effort and pain wipes the knife handle clean of finger-prints.*] Hurry away, Peter.

[PETER *begins to stagger away.*]

Wait . . . wait, Peter. Take your book . . . book. Right here . . . beside me . . . on your bench . . . my bench, rather. Come . . . take your book.

[PETER *starts for the book, but retreats.*]

Hurry . . . Peter.

[PETER *rushes to the bench, grabs the book, retreats.*]

Very good, Peter. . . . very good. Now . . . hurry away.

[PETER *hesitates for a moment, then flees, stage-left.*]

Hurry away . . . [*His eyes are closed now.*] Hurry away, your parakeets are making the dinner . . . the cats . . . are setting the table . . .

PETER [*off-stage, a pitiful howl*]: OH MY GOD!

JERRY [*his eyes still closed, he shakes his head and speaks; a combination of scornful mimicry and supplication*]: Oh . . . my . . . God. [*He is dead.*]

CURTAIN

*Some other Penguin plays
are described on the
following pages*

In One Volume

EPITAPH FOR GEORGE DILLON
John Osborne and Anthony Creighton

Epitaph for George Dillon was written by John Osborne in collaboration with Anthony Creighton before *Look Back in Anger*, the play which brought him to fame. Dillon himself is an earlier, more complex Jimmy Porter, viewed perhaps with a more critical eye than his successor. The play has been called 'the most wholly satisfactory of the plays Osborne has worked on'.

THE KITCHEN
Arnold Wesker

In *The Kitchen* Arnold Wesker presents, as a microcosm of the world, the stifling hell of an overcrowded restaurant kitchen. The bustle of the waitresses, the frenzy of the cook, leads tensely to an unexpected climax of horror and violence. *The Kitchen* was first presented at the Royal Court in 1959 and later filmed.

THE HAMLET OF STEPNEY GREEN
Bernard Kops

The Hamlet of Stepney Green was Bernard Kops's first play and one of the most highly praised of the dramas which followed on *Look Back in Anger*. The story of a twentieth-century Hamlet, a dreamer with ambitions as a crooner, it draws on Jewish traditions to produce an unaffected poetic folk-drama.

In One Volume

THE LONG AND THE SHORT AND THE TALL
Willis Hall

With Willis Hall's *The Long and the Short and the Tall* the 'Kitchen Sink' school of drama took a leap in time and space and brought the new toughness of approach to bear on an episode in the Malayan jungle-fighting of the Second World War. First produced on the 'fringe' of the Edinburgh Festival, the play was presented at the Royal Court in 1959 and was later filmed.

THE DUMB WAITER
Harold Pinter

The Dumb Waiter had its first production in Hamburg, before the critical and commercial success of *The Caretaker* in 1960 had established Pinter as one of the leading British playwrights. Written for two gunmen and a dumb waiter, it is an excellent example of Pinter's unnerving 'comedy of menace'.

A RESOUNDING TINKLE
N. F. Simpson

A Resounding Tinkle, like N. F. Simpson's other plays, fits into no category of drama in this age or any other. Inspired nonsense in a domestic setting, its most respectable ancestors are probably Edward Lear and the Goons.

FAIRY TALES OF NEW YORK

J. P. Donleavy

J. P. Donleavy's *Fairy Tales of New York* was first produced at the Pembroke Theatre, Croydon, with a cast of four actors. It was an immediate success and Donleavy received the *Evening Standard* Most Promising Playwright Award. Milton Shulman wrote of it: 'The writing is witty and sharp, the characters are brilliantly observed and the situations ping with authenticity.' Kenneth Tynan and the other critics were equally enthusiastic and the play was transferred complete with cast to the Comedy Theatre in January 1961.

The author was born in New York in 1926. His first novel, *The Ginger Man*, was published in Paris and later in England. A play was made from it. J. P. Donleavy lives, with his wife and two children, in London.

Three Plays by Eugène Ionesco

RHINOCEROS
THE CHAIRS
THE LESSON

Twelve years ago the plays of Ionesco, a Rumanian by origin, were being acted in Left Bank theatres in Paris and very poorly attended. Now regarded as one of the most important writers of the *avant-garde*, he has a world-wide reputation and his plays are translated into many languages.

Sir Laurence Olivier took the leading part in *Rhinoceros* when it was produced in London in 1960 at the Royal Court Theatre, where *The Chairs* had already been performed in 1957. *The Lesson* was produced at London's Arts Theatre Club in 1955.

Ionesco himself is hesitant to theorize about his work or assess its importance. His plays represent, he says, 'a mood and not an ideology, an impulse not a programme'. The substance of the world seems to vary, for him, between solidity and illusory unreality and he projects on to the stage, with a strangely universal effect of comedy, his own internal conflict.

His influence can be traced among the youngest generation of English playwrights.

For a complete list of books available please write to Penguin Books whose address can be found on the back of the title page